When GOD Calls

© 2021 by TGS International, a wholly owned subsidiary of Christian Aid Ministries, Berlin, Ohio.

All rights reserved. No part of this book may be reproduced or stored in any retrieval system, in any form or by any means, electronic or mechanical, without written permission from the publisher except for brief quotations embodied in critical articles and reviews.

ISBN: 978-1-63813-052-9

Revised edition

Cover and interior design: Kristi Yoder

Printed in the USA

Published by:
TGS International
P.O. Box 355
Berlin, Ohio 44610 USA
Phone: 330.893.4828
Fax: 330.893.2305
www.tgsinternational.com

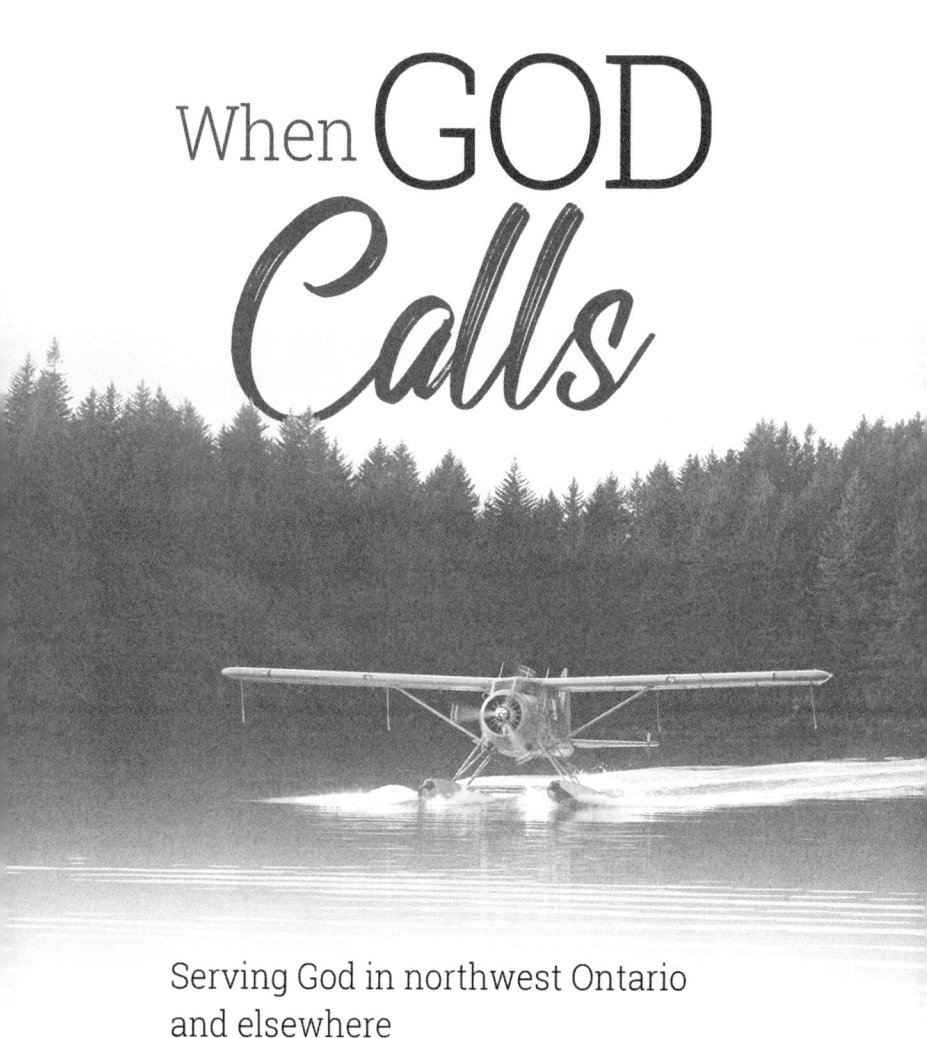

When GOD Calls

Serving God in northwest Ontario and elsewhere

Edwin Troyer

Table of Contents

Introduction 7
Part One: Trip to Brazil 11
  1. A Miracle 13
  2. To Brazil 21
  3. Identifying with Jonah 31
Part Two: Ministry in Slate Falls 39
  4. Heading North 41
  5. A Place Called Slate Falls 49
  6. Getting Settled 57
  7. The Violent Party 69

8. "Can You Help Me?"	77
9. Journey to Cat Lake	87
10. Memorable People	97
11. The Chase	107
12. Wilderness Surprise	117
13. Stranded!	125
14. A Powerful God	131
15. Alex	137
16. Incidents and Accidents	145

Part Three: Other Travel Adventures 153

17. An Unforgettable Trip	155
18. Visas for Romanians	163
Epilogue	169

Introduction

*O*ur friends have often encouraged us to write a book to share our experiences. This is the result of those requests. We are happy to share our stories of how the Lord has guided us and taught us in our mission work. We want to give all the honor and glory to God. As you read these pages, trust Him. He is the ultimate controller of all things.

This book is a three-part story of our family's journey in pursuing what we felt was the Lord's leading. He led us step by step, though many times we strayed from the path.

Part One is the story of the steps leading to our ministry in northwestern Ontario among the Ojibwe people. It tells of the flight on an old relic DC-3 and how the Lord preserved my life and the lives of the other passengers in a miraculous way. I hope this story confirms that God really does have a keen interest in protecting and guiding His children in unusual ways. For me, this experience brought my faith to a higher level.

It helped me come to the point that when obstacles appeared, I could tell myself, "Go ahead. God will work out something." The experience on the DC-3 flight and my time in the Amazon is what planted the seed and the desire to do mission work. However, mission work is not limited to living in a foreign land and adapting to a different culture. It is our daily walk of life, wherever we are, giving attention to the Holy Spirit's direction from day to day.

Part Two is the story of our family's calling to fulltime mission work in Canada and how we walked that journey step by step. God designs our journey not based on our interest and aptitude alone, but also on our willingness and faith, even when difficulties seem to overwhelm us. God doesn't require us to see the success of our endeavors. He only requires us to be faithful.

Finally, *Part Three* tells of some of our other travels and how God has continued to lead us to other parts of the world. We lived in Jerusalem for several months and have traveled through many countries, including Turkey, Greece, Romania, Moldova, Poland, England, Netherlands, Norway, Germany, France, Switzerland, Italy, Jordan, and Egypt.

My wife Edna and I grew up in caring, godly Amish homes in Holmes County, Ohio. Both of our fathers were ordained ministers. I was raised on a farm, and my father was a carpenter. I enjoyed working with Dad in our little shop where he made bedroom suites, grandfather clocks, and other furniture. Then, when I was twenty, I got a job in a cabinet shop. I worked in the kitchen cabinet business, intertwined with mission work, for a total of twenty-four years.

Our parents were always interested in missions and supported organizations that they felt were serving the Lord in Scriptural ways. They instilled in us a desire to serve the Lord and others, and we have tried to live our lives with that as our primary calling and focus. I am not pretending that we have arrived at the top of the ladder of faith, but we have hopefully gained a step or two.

I hope that as you read these pages, you will see how God leads us, protects us, and sustains us on our journey. He has certainly done that for us. I pray He will do the same for you.

Part One

Trip to Brazil

Chapter 1

A Miracle

*I*t was January 1974, and I was excited. My plans for a trip to Brazil finally seemed to be coming to fulfillment! I had been making plans for this journey for so long that I had often wondered if it would ever happen.

John Hostetler and his family, friends of ours, were long-term missionaries serving with Wycliffe Bible Translators in Brazil. They were now on furlough in our area and were asking for volunteers to go with them to the Wycliffe base in Belem, Brazil. The missionary families serving there lived in huts in the jungle just like the native Amazon people. But every six weeks or so, Wycliffe allowed them a short furlough to the base where they could rest and be rejuvenated.

The living quarters at the base were limited, so John was asking for help to build or remodel a small house for them to live in.

There were twenty-eight of us who volunteered to go on the trip—twenty-six men and two women. It took several months to get our necessary things together, including visas, tickets, and permits. Our plan was to leave from Miami, Florida. However, during the last few weeks before our departure, John heard about a chance to fly on an aircraft owned by the Smithsonian Institution in Washington, D.C. This service was offered to nonprofit organizations for no cost except paying the pilot. The plane was an older model but was supposedly in good condition. Since we were all happy to save some money, our group eagerly accepted the offer.

Before the trip, we faced some obstacles, including one big one that nearly eliminated me. Three weeks before our departure, I developed a serious flu-like sickness. The doctors finally diagnosed it as mononucleosis. Blood tests confirmed it as a tough case. The doctors told me it could take up to six months before I could do any work. I had a fever of up to 104 degrees and couldn't eat for days. I was too sick to care much about the trip, but we prayed and gave it over to the Lord, knowing that He is the Master Healer.

After a week of being very sick, I went to see the doctor again, feeling quite well. Miraculously, my blood tests showed up completely clear. "I don't know what you did," the doctor said. "But we see nothing that should hinder your trip to Brazil." Praise the Lord! I felt good, both physically and spiritually. I believe it was a direct healing from God.

Finally the day came. At 4:00 on the morning of January 2, 1974, we were eagerly waiting to board the plane to Brazil. As we looked at the plane, we started having some serious misgivings. It was a DC-3 twin-engine plane—an old one. But the most disturbing thing was its paint job of snakes, dragons, and other ghoulish figures. *What does it matter?* I thought. *Why worry about the paint on an airplane?*

There was a slight mist in the air, which we knew could quickly turn to ice if the temperature dropped a bit more. Ice on any aircraft, we knew, was dangerous, so we needed to get into the air as soon as possible.

We all found a seat, and the plane seemed as eager to go as we were. We hoped the pilots knew how to fly this antique aircraft. The plan was to fly nonstop from Akron-Canton to Miami, where we would refuel and then continue to Belem, Brazil. Lord willing, we expected to be at our destination by evening. As the plane rolled down the runway, everybody settled in, getting acquainted with the other people on the flight. The plane lifted off the runway, and before we knew it, we were in the air. We were airborne approximately twenty minutes when we felt the first "bump." Everyone noticed it. This was not a turbulence bump. It was the whole plane shuddering. It was still dark outside, and as we looked out the window we were shocked to see flames shooting from the left engine.

Things did not look good. Before we had much time to discuss it with each other, the copilot got up and made an announcement, "Ladies and gentlemen, we have a serious problem. If you can pray or sing, do so."

John got to his feet and suggested we sing "My Faith Looks Up to Thee." He led in prayer, and then each of us had our own personal prayers. By now the left engine was no longer shooting flames, but the right engine also didn't sound right. As we looked out the windows, it was easy to see we were losing altitude.

The pilot's wife had come along "just for the ride." She sat on the floor near the front of the airplane, covered herself with a blanket, and screamed. Evidently she was not a Christian and did not want to face death.

After the left engine quit sputtering and flaming, and the right engine began having similar problems, everything became mostly quiet. There was only the faint sputtering of the right engine and the noise of the wind as we glided through the air. We were all lost in our own personal thoughts. I looked out the window and was shocked to see how close the lights on the ground appeared. I remember thinking about my family—my wife Edna, my daughters Virginia and Phyllis, and our unborn baby. *We are expecting our third child,* I thought, *but I will never see the child. Why did God allow us to begin this journey only to face certain death?*

I estimated we would crash into the ground in approximately ten minutes, based on our rate of descent. It was still dark outside, and we were able to see lights on the ground. I had often wondered what it felt like to come face to face with death. I can honestly testify of a peace that I believe God grants in a time like this. It was a soul-searching experience for all of us. I wondered if the pilots would even attempt to land the plane. We were pretty close to the ground at this point, maybe a few hundred feet in the air. We did not hear anything more from the cockpit.

We were now almost to the ground and had no hope of a safe landing, although the left engine was now also sputtering again. Then, I think we all saw it—long rows of blue lights, like an airport runway directly below us. No attempt was made to circle or reposition our approach. We just landed! There was no taxiing, no adjusting the flaps, no sudden braking, no sounds on board. All of us were in awe at the obvious miracle from God.

After landing, we all just sat still and let our emotions go free. No one applauded or screamed. No one yelled "Praise the Lord!" This was a moment that belonged to God.

After about five minutes of meditation, we slowly deplaned. The pilots immediately went to the left engine and opened the outer cover. Oil drained out, spilling onto the tarmac. The engine had been running with almost no oil! The pilots asked us to gather while they explained what had happened. But first we all formed a circle and thanked the Lord for His miracle.

The Whole Story

We soon learned the whole story from the pilots. As was obvious, the DC-3 airplane was an older aircraft. It had recently been through major surgery. The right engine had just been installed. It was a reconditioned engine but supposedly like new. The left one had been overhauled but not broken in. During the flight from Washington, D.C., to Ohio, there hadn't been any problems. But after loading up in Akron, it was too much for the left engine, causing a breach in the oil system, thus the flames and backfiring. The engine got overheated and lost oil pressure, so the pilots stopped that engine, assuming one engine could get us somewhere to land.

While the pilots were doing what they could to stabilize the plane, they were also communicating with the control towers in both

Akron/Canton and Pittsburgh. Their first thought was that the best thing to do was to turn back and land in Akron, but communication from Akron revealed that we had just left the ground when a serious ice storm glazed the runway with ice. "Do not try to land in Akron," was the word from the control tower.

The Pittsburgh airport gave the approval to land there, so the DC-3 turned its nose toward Pittsburgh. But the pilots had barely set on that course when the right engine started sputtering because of the extra load it had to carry. They soon realized that we were descending at a rate that would never get us to Pittsburgh.

So far the pilot and copilot had been busily trying this and that, but now they knew there was little left to try. As we quietly cruised along, they fearfully looked down into the darkness and knew it would take a miracle from God to save us.

There was a small country runway in East Liverpool, Ohio, so radio Pittsburgh called this little airport, having little hope that anyone would answer the phone at this time of morning. Of all things, the night watchman heard the phone and answered it. After learning of the situation, he quickly turned on the runway lights. Radio Pittsburgh then informed our pilots, giving them landing instructions. The bad news was that at our rate of descent, we would not quite reach the airport until we crashed.

The pilots, not being practicing Christians, encouraged us to keep praying. We were well aware that things were serious, but we didn't know how serious. We didn't know there was an airstrip eleven miles ahead but that we were descending too rapidly to reach it.

The pilots were still frantically trying different ideas, with little success. The right engine continued to sputter along, but the left one was silent. The air traffic controllers advised them to try restarting the left engine, even if there was no oil pressure. They assumed it was likely seized up, but it was their only hope.

When the captain engaged the starter to start the left engine, to their amazement, the engine started! It didn't run smoothly, but it sputtered along, and with the right engine sputtering about the same, they were able to maintain enough altitude to keep us airborne for the eleven miles needed to get to the East Liverpool Airport.

Try Again

"What do we do now?" we all asked. Most of our group said without hesitation, "We will go home. Brazil can manage without us." Several offered to donate money to pay for the trip for anyone who chose to go. We finally decided to all go home and pray about it, and anyone who felt willing and led to go could drive to Miami the next day and fly on a commercial flight to Belem, Brazil.

When I got home that day, I don't think I was ever so glad to see my wife and children. I had frequently been on work projects, and my wife Edna was used to being alone at times. But she had had a heavy feeling when I left that morning and was not greatly surprised when she got the message.

With joy we thanked the Lord for His deliverance.

Chapter 2

To Brazil

*C*hoosing to head for Brazil the next day was not an easy decision for me. Even after discussing it with my father, one question kept coming back: Why did God stop our journey so abruptly? It seemed as if God didn't want us to go. But then I remembered how I had been healed of my illness. Finally I decided to go.

By the next morning there were twelve of us who were willing to head south. But now we faced another challenge. This was during a gas shortage, and it was difficult to get gas. During the entire drive to Miami, each time we came to a station there seemed to be some kind of restriction. Maybe it was a sign that said "Out of gas" or "Limit: eight gallons per vehicle." At a few gas stations, we explained the situation we were in and why we needed gas, and they said to fill up and take all we needed. As we traveled and experienced miracles along the way, our faith grew stronger, and we began to think God would do anything we needed.

It was a very tired group of twelve men that boarded the flight in Miami. We planned to fly to Bogota, Colombia, and from there to Belem, Brazil. As soon as I stepped on board the plane, I had to face my fears of flying. After we were airborne, every so often I would look at the engines and listen to make sure they were running properly. Our leader, John Hostetler, had brought all kinds of supplies along—things they needed but could not buy in Brazil. As we went through customs in Miami, everybody wondered how we would get cleared in Brazil with some of the strange things we were taking. You know the phrase, "They brought everything except the kitchen sink." Well, that was us.

It was late at night when we arrived in Brazil. Nervously we lined up with all our goods, watching our packages going slowly in front of us on a conveyer with an inspector at the other end. About that time, the inspector must have needed a bathroom break because he left in a great hurry—but he didn't stop the conveyer! As soon as our things had passed through, we loaded everything on a cart and wheeled it to a waiting cab. Then we headed for the Wycliffe headquarters.

At the headquarters, we all found a place to rest our tired bodies—some on hammocks and some on thin mats on the floor. A few even had a couch to sleep on. I believe we all slept a little except for John. He was the leader and felt a load of responsibility.

Sometime in the wee hours of the morning, I woke with a jerk. Someone, or something, was yelling, "Lobel! Lobel!" *What in the world?* Then I heard it again. It sounded like someone was just outside my window. *Who is Lobel?* I wondered. John had said we would have a house all by ourselves with no other people around. It was still dark and not yet time to get up.

Soon we were all awake, and John showed up too. He apologized, saying he forgot to tell us about their parrot. Every morning the parrot would call their dog, whose name was Lobel.

Our next challenge was to silence the parrot. Shooting the bird was not an option, so someone suggested prayer. We tried that and decided God must be busy with other things. None of us got much more sleep that morning. For the rest of our stay, however, we did solve it, to a degree. The one who slept closest to the window where Lobel slept armed himself with bread crusts. Then when the parrot started his morning serenading, the person in charge would feed him bread crusts until he settled down again.

Getting Started

John was on the warpath to get some work out of us, but we all felt quite sluggish that first morning. So much had happened the last few days that we wanted to just sit and think about all the things we had experienced. The unsuccessful DC-3 flight and the uncertainty of whether or not we should continue the trip was a lot to process. Those of us who had decided to continue, despite our fears, felt we were doing the right thing.

On the first day we took a little tour of the Wycliffe community in Belem, Brazil. This is the base for the Bible translators who are living in remote regions of the Amazon jungles. There were probably fifteen to twenty neat little houses in this area, providing a place for the translators to live when they came to the base.

Every six months or so, the translators would take a break from life in the jungle and come to the base to be refreshed. Also, some of the work related to translation could be done more efficiently in a setting where there were fewer distractions. In the jungle, the natives had much time on their hands and would sometimes sit in a missionary's hut all day, assuming that they had lots of spare time. This often kept the missionaries from their work, so they were grateful to be able to escape to the city.

After getting acquainted with the area, we were given our assignments. I had worked much of my life making kitchen cabinets, so my job was to build kitchen cabinets in a new house they were building.

I wasn't sure what to think when I was shown the lumber I was to use. We just drove around on a four-wheeler and picked up a board here and there. We found some boards lying under a building, and some were even submerged in water! "This is your lumber," I was told. "If you need more, we will bring you some."

I was used to working with fine grade lumber, so I immediately knew this would be much different. The man who helped me find the lumber soon raced off, and I wondered what I had gotten myself into. The tools I had been given were a hammer, a measuring tape, a hand saw, a saber saw, and a handful of nails! Being all alone, I had no one to complain to about my situation. I just had to build a kitchen!

When midday came, someone rounded us up and took us to a little house where a middle-aged couple had cooked a meal for us. After lunch we lounged around a bit. I spread out on the grass until somebody hollered at me, "Don't lie on the grass! There are millions of chiggers. There are also snakes—and many of them are poisonous!"

Soon we heard a few claps of thunder, and then the rain came tumbling down. "I forgot to tell you that we are in the rainy season," John told us. "Every day it rains for about fifteen minutes, then it will be hot and humid for the rest of the day."

After the sudden shower was over, we all went back to work. When I started to cut some lumber I discovered it to be extremely hard. I almost considered asking our mechanic to come and weld the boards together! I realized, however, that this was not a good idea.

Thus began our initiation to life in Brazil. It seemed to get hotter every day, and the humidity must have been close to 95 percent.

To the Jungle

After about a week, John told our group one morning that he was looking for a way to fly to a jungle village where missionaries Ed and Sally Kahn had lived for fifteen years. They had some work they needed help with, and this would give us a taste of what the jungle was like. John said the only way to get to the interior was with the Brazilian air force, which had been making some practice flights deep into the Amazon jungle. If there was any room left on board, civilians were sometimes allowed to fly with them. Personally, I wasn't sure how many more "practice flights" I could endure. But since the rest of the group seemed eager to try it, I pretended to be eager as well.

When John went to the military base to see if it would work out, an officer picked up a clipboard of names, looked over the top of his glasses, then muttered, "Look, I have thirty names on the waiting list. There is no way to get you on board." I didn't know whether to be relieved or disappointed.

We were almost ready for lunch when John came with more news. He had received a call from the military. They told him if we could be at the air force base the next morning at seven o'clock, we could ride along. This brought some new energy to our group. This was truly another miracle from God. We were almost getting used to having solid answers to our prayers.

John said it would be an eight-hour flight on a Buffalo plane. *What is a Buffalo plane?* I wondered. *Do they fly buffaloes?*

They normally flew the plane west along the Amazon River to the end of the jungle, and then the next day they would return to the base in Belem. We decided that everyone would go along, but then only six of us would return to Belem the next day when the plane returned. The other half of the crew would stay with Ed and Sally Kahn for about two weeks. There wasn't enough work for all of us to do, nor were there adequate facilities to house all of us.

On the flight back to Belem, they told us, the military flight crew would first fly to a small air force base where they would spend the night. This place was only a tent camp, but we could use our hammocks if we wanted to. Then the next morning we would board the Buffalo plane and return late that evening. The plan seemed acceptable to us.

The next morning there was quite a bustle while we figured out what to take along on the journey. Obviously, the six of us who were coming back to Belem needed fewer items than those who would be in the jungle for two weeks. I had a small backpack with only the bare necessities.

When we arrived at the airport, we saw an airplane on the runway, apparently the one we would be traveling on. It barely resembled an airplane. It had a very long wingspan, with the wings positioned approximately eight feet above the fuselage. At the end of each wing was a small pontoon, and the belly of the craft looked like one big float. As we sized it up, it was easy to see that it was an amphibious aircraft, able to land on both land and water. With the DC-3 experience still fresh in our minds, we were concerned how clumsy and old it looked. We wondered what we were getting into.

We had no time to back out of our commitment. We simply had to trust the Lord that all would be well. As we boarded the strange-looking bird, we discovered that the inside looked even more questionable than the outside. The seating consisted of long benches along the wall. There were exposed wires, cables, and ropes that supposedly controlled the functions of the airplane. Anyone feeling mischievous could easily have pulled some "strings" and taken over the plane from the convenience of the cabin area!

There were military officers scattered throughout the cabin, not because of security but because they needed a place to sit. I could easily endorse the idea of making "practice runs" through the jungle. It appeared these folks really did need practice!

We were finally speeding down the runway in a slow, lumbering way. We all kept our eyes on the upcoming trees of the jungle. Finally the plane left the ground. The pilots flew the plane in a big circle, but I could tell we were losing altitude. To gain momentum, they dropped down while racing the engines, just narrowly missing the treetops. They did the same thing over the river, dropping down and splashing the water, then climbing back up again. Finally, to everyone's relief, we had enough speed to stay aloft.

Another troubling thing was the landing procedure. When we started our descent, one soldier grabbed a sledgehammer and crawled on his belly under the pilots' seats. His job was to whack the landing gear on the nose. Apparently it was usually stuck and needed some persuasion.

After eight hours of white-knuckle flying, we landed in the village where Ed and Sally Kahn were living among the natives, learning their language and creating an alphabet for them. These were people who could not read or write and had probably never seen a Bible.

We had barely enough time to walk through the little village where the Kahns lived before it was time for our group to separate. It had not really dawned on us that when we left the village where Ed and Sally lived we would be on our own with the military. Not one of the six of us could speak more than a handful of Portuguese words. We waved goodbye to the others and took off on the short flight to where we would be staying for the night.

A Primitive Village

When we circled in preparation for landing, we could see a small village of bamboo huts close to the air force base. The officers who operated the flight were very friendly, and after we landed they did their best to show us where we belonged. We understood that supper would be served in one of the tent facilities a few hours later. After traveling all day and being under severe stress—or maybe fear—we were eager to unwind, so we decided to explore the little village. We were surprised to see well-traveled trails through the jungle.

Seeing this jungle village was like entering a different world. The natives' homes were nothing more than three-sided huts made of bamboo poles and thatched roofs. To our relief, the people seemed friendly enough. They were adorned with jewelry in their ears and noses and wore hardly any clothes. The women wore a small apron hanging from a string around their waist, and the men also wore nothing but a leather loincloth.

As we walked around, we found it very interesting to see how they lived. At one place they were cooking supper. The menu that night was roasted monkey. They held the monkeys by the tail over the fire until they were scorched black. They did not offer us a taste—nor did we ask for any!

Exploring this jungle tribe was both humbling and fascinating. In an entirely new way, I saw the need for missionaries to do what Wycliffe was doing. As we left the village, I had many questions. Have these people ever heard of Jesus Christ? What form of religion do they have? How is God going to judge these people? It seemed so unfair that we have so much. Above all, that we have the Gospel drilled into us at a very young age.

I cannot explain my emotions as we left this little village in the Amazon jungle to walk back to the air force base. Just beyond the last hut, I turned and looked back. To my right, I saw children playing in the dirt, completely naked. They had probably never seen a bathtub. The sun was setting in the west just as it did everywhere else in the world. I wondered if my family in Ohio was looking at the same sun. I also wondered if the people we had just seen would hear the Gospel before the sun set on their lives.

That was probably the moment and the place where I personally renewed my commitment to serve the Lord in a deeper way and committed my life to serve Him in missions.

Chapter 3

Identifying with Jonah

The air force station was a tent camp occupied by soldiers. There were no civilians around, so we felt rather alone. We knew that John had explained to the soldiers that we would sleep in their camp tonight, and then in the morning continue on the flight back to Belem.

It was dusk, but it didn't seem dark enough to go to bed, so we meandered around the camp. We noticed there was a cook tent where the soldiers were cooking their dinner. The odors coming from the tent were quite tantalizing. I suppose anything would have been tempting considering we had not eaten all day. Even roasted monkey was starting to sound good. Soon one of the officers came over and motioned for us to come and eat with them. No argument there. We quickly went to a table in the cook tent. I don't remember what we ate, but it was good.

Then we noticed a group of officers standing in a little huddle, talking and looking in our direction. We wondered if we had done something wrong. One of the officers came to our table, put his hands on the edge, and started talking to us. We had no clue what he was saying. The only answer we had for him was, "No comprendo," though that was no doubt obvious!

We could literally see the frustration building in the officer. He went and solicited another officer to come and communicate with these strange men. No success! They then took us on a little walk up a small hill and around a bend where there was a more stylish tent. Inside, sitting behind a desk, was an officer who was obviously of high rank. He was very friendly and spoke English quite well. He raised no fuss, he just let us know that there were sick people who needed to go to the hospital tomorrow—so there would be no room for us on the plane.

He could see by our expressions that this was not what we wanted to hear. He assured us that we should not be troubled, for in approximately two weeks they would fly in again. What a consolation!

The officer then hastened to tell us that there actually was room on the plane for us to fly partway—until we got to the village where they would pick up the sick people. I tried to remember the verse "Let not your heart be troubled: ye believe in God, believe also in me" (John 14:1).

It was time for another prayer meeting.

We went a short distance away and gathered in a circle. Once again we called on God to help us know what to do. It seemed like we were always asking God what we should do, but so far He had been generous in answering our prayers. We looked up at the stars and the moon, wondering if God had everything under control. Then we stood in a circle and sang "How Great Thou Art."

It had been a long day. We thought of the miracles we had seen and how God was taking care of us. Now all we could do was hang up our hammocks, get some sleep, and hope that after a good night's rest, God would work out something.

To Another Village

The next morning all six of us were down at the river next to our Buffalo plane. There would be no chance of them leaving without us. After about an hour, the pilots showed up, along with several other people we had not seen the day before.

One of the new people on the flight was a white man who spoke excellent English. He introduced himself and said he was an anthropologist and was doing some studies about various people groups all over the world. We tried to explain what we were doing. He told us he was an atheist and didn't need to worry about pleasing Jesus or God. But then he asked, "Isn't there a verse in the Bible that says Jesus won't return until everybody in the whole world has learned about Him?" We assured him there was such a verse and that we believed it was true.[1]

He was a giant of a man—six feet four inches, at least. But size

---

[1] See Matthew 24:14

Identifying with Jonah

is not everything, we soon learned. During our conversation, he paused, and I realized he was crying. "If you believe this," he said, "why don't you leave some villages so Jesus does not come?" It was obvious that this man's theology did not give him any security in times of trouble.

By this time, the pilots and crew were getting the Buffalo ready to travel. We forgot our manners and crowded in first to get a seat. We didn't care if it was a good seat—any seat would do. We felt rather smug as we raced down the runway. Maybe the general's news was a false alarm. Maybe they would forget that we were on board. Maybe we could just sit still when we got to the next village and we wouldn't get left behind. We soon saw that they were preparing to land when the fellow with the sledgehammer crawled under the pilots' seats to hammer the nose wheel. When we landed, we all sat quietly with our eyes closed, hoping nobody would notice us. It didn't work. An officer soon came and motioned us to get off the plane.

This air force compound was a bit more civilized. They had a few trucks, which indicated that it was accessible by some kind of road, probably during the dry season. It was certainly not a very populated place though. It was now midmorning, and the sun was doing its best. To our dismay, we soon observed people boarding the plane. We were a rather somber little group as we watched the Buffalo race down the runway without us. Seeing a little picket fence a short distance away, we sat down with our backs against it to rest our tired bodies.

As we watched, we saw a mixture of native and non-native people, but none who could speak English. After about an hour of roasting ourselves and having people looking at us inquisitively, we began to realize how animals felt in a zoo. It was starting to soak in that we might be here for a long time. There we sat, with no food, water, or shelter. I couldn't help but wonder if this was how Jonah felt when his shade tree fell apart.

Sometime later we heard the sound of an airplane coming in to land on the airstrip. It was a nice, newish looking airplane, painted in beautiful, fresh colors. When it stopped not too far from where we were sitting, we noticed it was a DC-3. Our minds immediately went to our DC-3 experience two weeks earlier. It actually seemed more like two years. We decided this must be somebody important the way the plane looked and how the officers were dressed in their finest military uniforms.

But we weren't impressed. We just went back to our picket fence and sat in the sand, acting just like Jonah. Finally someone asked the question we were all tormented with: "Do you think anybody will ever find us? Nobody even knows we are here. We will probably die here."

As we sat there sweltering in the sun, I had more and more admiration for Jonah—and we were every bit as pessimistic as he was! A few minutes later we saw a man coming our way. He looked like an American. "Hello," he said, greeting us with a smile and speaking fluent English, "I am a missionary in a neighboring village."

He was indeed an American missionary serving with Missionary Alliance Church in a small Indian village about twenty miles away. He had lived there for ten years.

There were no vehicles where he lived, so one of the soldiers had driven a vehicle as far as he could and then walked the remaining miles to see if the missionary would come and interpret for us. They were desperate to find out who we were and what we wanted.

There was some activity over close to where the plane had landed, so the missionary went with us to see what was going on. They were having some kind of government dedication ceremony that involved high-ranking officials of the government, including the brigadier general. He had flown in on his own private airplane. We felt quite honored to see him.

The missionary explained to the officers that we needed a ride to Belem. Walking wasn't an option because it was four hundred miles away.

When the missionary left, we went back to our little spot in the sun with the realization that nothing had actually changed. We were still lost, we were still hungry and thirsty, and we were still in need of a shower. The missionary had given us some hope, however, and we were not quite as pessimistic as before. And the Brazilian air force soldiers no longer had that perplexed look on their faces.

God Makes a Way

A short time later, a young soldier headed our direction. He seemed eager to tell us something. Of course, communication was still with "signs and wonders"—we made the signs and they wondered. But his signs were unmistakable. He was saying, "Come with me!" We needed no second invitation. We followed him all the way to that beautiful DC-3 airplane, and he motioned for us to get on and find a seat. We obeyed, but we were puzzled and surprised. Surely we would not be traveling with such a high-ranking officer. We waited quite a while and it was getting hot inside, but we certainly did not intend to get off the plane.

Finally the ceremony seemed to be finished, and the officers began coming our way and boarding the plane. It would be difficult to describe either their expressions or ours. We looked about as ragtag as Amish and Mennonite men can after two long days of being dragged around without showers, Right Guard, and food. But the twin engines of the DC-3 were now running. We listened carefully for any unusual sounds that might emit from the engines but were overjoyed to be moving, going somewhere. We didn't know where, but that was beside the point. It was once again a miracle in the making. God was in charge. Why did we so soon forget?

After about an hour and a half, we noticed we were landing. We still did not know where, but we soon decided this must be Belem.

When we had safely landed and deplaned, we discovered that the brigadier general had flown the plane himself, just for the fun of it. When we shook his hand and thanked him for the ride, we discovered that he spoke English quite well.

Someone from the flight crew contacted the Wycliffe base and told them to come pick us up. The local people in the Wycliffe base were shocked. Never had they heard of civilians flying with the brigadier general. But with God all things are possible. "Lord, forgive us for having Jonah attitudes."

. . . .

Looking back, we often had the question: Why did God stop the DC-3 flight from Akron? We have since learned that the painting on the original plane depicted an Indian religion practiced in some of the villages we planned to visit. That would have carried the wrong message to the people we wanted to point to Christ.

And perhaps there is another reason. The rest of our group who stayed behind in Ed and Sally Kahn's village had services in the evening for the tribal natives living there. One day a native from another village across the mountain stopped in to visit. He stayed several days and heard the Gospel message of Jesus Christ. He was converted and went back home to his village and shared the Gospel. Many accepted Jesus, and the last we heard there is a thriving Christian church there. God has amazing ways to accomplish His work.

For me and my family, this trip opened our eyes to the needs of spreading the Gospel. Although being a missionary in a different culture sometimes has its twists and turns, we will never be happier than where God calls us.

Part Two

Ministry in Slate Falls

Chapter 4

Heading North

*O*ne beautiful fall day I heard a car pull into our driveway. A stranger stepped out, came to our front door, and knocked. When I opened the door, he politely introduced himself.

"Hello. I am Tom Hingson," he said. "I am with a company called Tower Communications, based in Texas. We are in the process of building a string of cell phone towers across the United States, and we found that a property owned by Edwin Troyer has the highest elevation in this area. We would like to lease a spot on your hill to erect a tower."

He went on to say that it would require access to an area of approximately three acres. He asked if I would be willing to lease a spot on our land to build a cell phone tower. I politely said we were probably not interested but would give it some thought.

Before he returned to his car, he turned around and said, "You are probably curious how much we would pay for such a project." He then proceeded to tell me what the company would offer in monthly payments.

After he left, my wife and I discussed it. All at once it dawned on me: the amount he quoted was almost the exact amount of our mortgage payments for our farm—and for the exact number of years of our mortgage!

After my miraculous trip to Brazil, we had a keen sense that there is more to life than just working to achieve the American Dream—more than just owning a comfortable home and raising a family. We sensed a call to go somewhere for mission work and had committed ourselves to be willing, but we weren't sure how we could do it. Our prayer was, "Lord, if you show us how to be financially able to go, we will go." Now, as we considered the tower proposal, we realized that God was answering that prayer. We discussed it with our parents and decided if God was trying to get our attention, we had better listen.

We had no clear feeling where we should go. We had once made a trip to Canada and enjoyed what we saw in the north. Discussing the various options, we all felt we didn't want to be stuck in some "back in the bush" location with our family.

We had heard of a residential school in Poplar Hill, Ontario—operated by Northern Light Gospel Missions. Poplar Hill was a fly-in reserve, but there were usually quite a few people coming and going. This appealed to us and seemed to make sense for our family.

Northern Light Gospel Missions was headquartered in Red Lake,

Ontario, under the leadership of lrvin Schantz, who started it in the early 1960s. Irvin and a few other men from Pennsylvania had a vision to serve the natives in northwestern Ontario. At this time there were approximately twelve Indian reserves in that area. It was the vision of the mission leadership to provide a resident missionary couple/family for every reserve. Red Lake was the logical location for their headquarters because that is where the natives went to buy supplies. All of these reserves were dependent on floatplanes to bring in supplies.

We notified the mission that we would prefer a location where our family could be among other people. We were assured there would be an opening, but then the organization kept suggesting a reserve called Slate Falls that really needed a resident couple to do ministry work. Our answer was always no, not with a family. But more and more, the mission leaders were hoping we would change our minds and be willing to serve at Slate Falls.

Several months rolled by as we slowly made preparations for a possible move. Up to that point, our church had not given us a clear answer if we should go or not, but then the day came when our church gave us full consent to go. A representative from Northern Light called us the following morning and said there was no longer an opening at Poplar Hill. He asked again if we would consider going to Slate Falls. I answered, "Today our answer is yes, but if you had called last week it would still have been no. Now, with the consent of the church just yesterday, we are willing to go wherever you suggest."

Henry, the mission representative, then told me that he tried calling us the week before but could not get through. This was another confirmation that God was working on this project. How could we refuse?

Our answer to Northern Light Gospel Missions had become clear. A bush village named Slate Falls was where God was calling us to serve. There was still much preparation. We needed to pack all our supplies, get our house ready for renters, and make arrangements for our absence.

Finally, however, we were ready to move north.

On the Way

The rain pelted the roof of the van. It was loaded with my precious family and enough provisions to last for who knows how long. I sat in the back seat, hoping my wife and children would not see the tears flowing from my eyes.

Was I really doing the right thing, taking my family 1,300 miles north into bush country to a place we had never seen? We had never even seen pictures of Slate Falls. *Slate Falls, Slate Falls, Slate Falls . . .* The name sounded nice. I wondered if there was a big waterfall—something like Niagara Falls. Soon the rain began to beat harder, and the day became even drearier. Everyone else in the van seemed to be asleep except the driver and my niece Yvonne, who had come along for the ride.

According to the road signs, we were approaching Chicago. I wondered if this was the point of no return. My thoughts continued to churn. In the busyness of getting packed and the excitement of going, there had been no time to reflect or reconsider. Now I found myself doing nothing but that.

My thoughts went to the dramatic experience I had after boarding the DC-3 for Brazil. I relived the terrifying minutes and rejoiced in how God had performed an amazing miracle. My thoughts then went to that remote jungle village along the Amazon, and I remembered how I had felt the call to serve somewhere.

The rain continued—as did the tears, the thoughts, and the doubts. Was the Tower Communications deal perhaps just a coincidence? How could I be sure God was in all of this and it wasn't just my stubborn thirst for adventure? Circumstances happen to everyone, right? No answer. "God, are you listening? Or don't you even care?"

Silence, except for the whir of the wheels, which kept rolling farther and farther from Holmes County. The children kept snoozing from the sheer exhaustion of the past weeks and months. By late afternoon, we passed Chicago and were soon in the rolling terrain of southern Wisconsin. The rain had finally ceased. The tears too had subsided, and my thoughts were more settled. I would trust God and go forth in faith. I would trust that God is in control, and that right now, on June 9, 1981, this was where God wanted us.

No Room for Hitchhikers

I felt a twinge of amusement as I looked around the van. Behind me, beside me—everywhere—were boxes and bags of all descriptions—not to mention all the pillows and blankets. Everything was piled helter-skelter to the roof. In and among all this was my dear wife, who had submitted herself to go where I would go, and our three children.

Our oldest daughter, Virginia Ruth, was getting to be a young lady.

She was now fourteen years old and as skinny as a rail, which is why her schoolmates called her "Skinny Ginny." Along the side of the van, with her head buried in a pillow, was our second born, Phyllis Noreen. She was ten years old, loved working outdoors with me, and was always willing to try anything. She was named after several native Indian girls we had met some years earlier.

Our youngest child, our only son, was hidden somewhere under all the rubble. Jeremy Lynn was six years old and had little clue where we were going. He had already had his share of adventures in his short life and was eager for more. His cute little cowlick identified him as Edwin's son. He had inclinations of becoming a mechanic, but he did have a few things to learn yet. I couldn't help but think of the time he had used a water hose to fill the fuel tank of our lawn mower instead of using gasoline. It was a great idea that unfortunately didn't work. There was also the time he was playing on the farm tractor and slid the shift lever out of gear. Since it was parked on a hill, he got a thrilling ride as it coasted down a slope.

Slowly the family started to wake up with stomachs growling. Somebody noticed that there was a McDonald's up ahead. We knew that where we were going there would be no McDonald's, so McDonald's it was!

Everyone seemed happy and cheerful. Our driver, Carolyn, was especially enjoying the bright sunshine after fighting traffic in rain through Chicago. I purposed to "leave it all behind" and be happy in trusting God's leading. The road wound on around lakes and through forests, ever northward. It was beautiful, but there was so much of it! At one filling station, the attendant peeked inside the van and said, "It looks rather cozy in there!"

After two days of driving, we were happy to see a sign pointing to the left: RED LAKE, 125 km. We thought we had seen all the beauty of the north, but the landscape in this area was even prettier. The shimmering water of pristine lakes under bright blue skies was unbelievably beautiful.

Occasionally we saw black bears. One of the cutest scenes was a mama bear with three cubs right along the highway. When we stopped, Mama Bear quickly communicated to her cute little children that this was potential danger. Quick as a flash, they scurried up a tree, all three at different heights, and peeked out from behind the trunk. Mama Bear planted herself on her rear in front of the tree, oblivious to the curiosity of her children. Her language was distinctly clear: "Don't even *think* of harming my babies!"

Chapter 5

A Place Called Slate Falls

The wheels of our van kept rolling north. By this time, Holmes County seemed far away. The "old" had dissipated into the cool northern air, and the "new" looked interesting and exciting. We somewhat knew what to expect in Red Lake, as we had visited friends in this small northern city approximately fourteen years earlier. Red Lake was the jumping-off place for all the native people living in the reserves or bush villages farther north. The only way to travel to these other villages was by floatplanes. We were excited to think that in several days one of these floatplanes would carry our family to the little village of Slate Falls, where our new life would begin. Little was thought and less was said about Holmes County, Ohio, which we had left behind. The anticipation of new adventures took over, and we were happily disengaged from the pressures of our home community.

After the original founders of Northern Light Gospel Missions had established Red Lake as their headquarters, they hired privately owned airplanes to transport them hundreds of miles north, east, and west to other remote areas where the natives lived. They ultimately developed a system where Northern Light Gospel Missions had missionary families living in nearly all the northern reserves, of which Slate Falls was one of them.

As the mission grew, it eventually became necessary to have their own aircraft and pilots. Through generous donations from the States, Northern Light now owned six planes. Cessna produced a plane that performed very well in the harsh environment of northern Ontario, so when we arrived in 1981, the mission's main workhorses were the Cessna 180 and 185. These were four- and five-seaters and flew much faster than the older radial engine planes.

In addition to the three Cessnas, the mission also owned a Swiss-made aircraft called a Pilatus Porter. This aircraft could carry seven people besides the pilot. The Pilatus was a slow workhorse with a very long wingspan, giving it a reputation for short takeoffs and landings.

When we arrived at the Northern Light headquarters, I saw a map on the wall showing northwestern Ontario. The Indian reserves that had resident missionaries were highlighted, showing that they were represented. I then noticed one community marked with a different color. The caption read "Slate Falls—Troyer family coming soon."

Once a year, Northern Light would host a conference when all the "bush missionaries" would come to Red Lake for a time of socializing, getting acquainted, and spiritual refreshment. Sometimes there were even ball games. Approximately twelve to fifteen families were now in Red Lake for this annual event. We had arrived just in time to get acquainted with the whole "mission family." It was truly a stretching experience for our family.

As we fellowshipped with other families who had lived on reserves for up to ten years and heard their experiences, I wondered if we would ever encounter things like that. And if we did, would we be able to handle it? I had imagined native people to be shy, subdued, and quiet. I thought they all lived in little cabins and went fishing every day. But this was not what we were hearing from our newfound friends. It sounded more like we were in for long days spiked with unexpected events and even scary situations with intoxicated locals. They told us there would be little time for leisure.

Of course, I wasn't planning to be lazy; I knew it would be hard work. But the more I heard, the more intimidated I felt. Were we really equipped for this? Were we at the right place? Were we sure about those "leadings"? Was I unnecessarily exposing my dear family to spiritual dangers? The thoughts persisted. The thought of turning around and going back home was a humiliating one!

We had two beautiful days of fellowship and fine weather with our mission family. The more we became acquainted with the team of mission personnel, the more the feelings of doubt dissipated into the northern air. Then it was time to release our driver and Yvonne to go back home. There were tears—good, healthy tears— as we said our goodbyes, but the time had come to get to the work that God had called us. We were thankful to feel much more ready to face whatever that might be.

Home Sweet Home

Before we were ready to fly to our new home in Slate Falls, we had to take care of a few necessities—things like taking part in orientations and establishing bank accounts. By the time we were ready to load our belongings onto the Pilatus aircraft, a weather front moved in and there was no flying weather for three days. By this time, we were all eager to go.

Every mission station under Northern Light had a two-way radio for communicating with Red Lake headquarters. The pilots were continually calling other stations to check on their weather to get a feel of when the weather pattern would clear. Occasionally someone would call Irvin Schantz at headquarters and ask, "How is your weather?" And Irvin would answer, "We've got lots of it!"

Some of the native people from Slate Falls seemed as eager to see us as we were to meet them. They kept calling every day to find out when these new "white people" were coming. Finally the day came when Leonard, one of the main pilots, decided this was the day. The weather was still on the iffy side, but we were eager to go, and I suspect the mission staff at Red Lake headquarters was just as ready to see us going.

After every nook and cranny of the airplane was stuffed full of our luggage, we were told to get on board. Once we were all strapped in, they piled more things on our laps. There was no possibility of bouncing around in there! We taxied out to the middle of the lake to warm up the engine. Finally we lined up for a straight course across the lake and headed into the wind for takeoff. The plane was loaded so heavily that the pontoons were nearly buried in the water. But the bush pilots knew exactly what they were doing, and we had full trust in their skills. The aircraft labored and muddled through the water for the first one hundred feet, then it started to pick up speed and gradually lifted out of the water. We were on our way! What an exhilarating feeling to look down on the treetops!

The children were all eyes for the first thirty minutes. After that, though the scenery was beautiful, it all started to look the same. When we had flown for nearly an hour, Leonard pointed straight ahead, and we got our first glimpse of Slate Falls. It looked kind of like we expected—a dozen little log cabins nestled in the trees and scattered along the lake. When we got down lower, we could see boats on the water and people walking on narrow footpaths, all headed toward one house in particular. I decided that must be our house—the mission house. We circled the village several times to make our grand arrival known to all.

As we taxied to the dock, the natives came out of the bush from everywhere. Eager hands, large and small, were pushing and shoving to be the first to grab hold of the airplane and tie it securely to the dock. The mission house was just up the bank. These were our premises, our home. There was no time to figure out if we liked it because there were so many other things to do. With lots of help, we began unloading all our things and carrying everything to the house.

It had been nearly four months since anyone had lived in the house. The first missionaries to set foot in Slate Falls came in 1955. They were Allen Sommers and his wife Emma, who was my cousin. They came as genuine pioneers. In fact, they lived in a tent the first summer. The house that we were to live in had been built only three years earlier.

Compared to many of the houses in native villages, this house was luxurious. We even had kitchen cupboards with a stainless-steel sink, complete with a drain that led outside to a sort of leach bed. Since there was no running water, there was also no toilet.

However, in a little room behind the kitchen was a wooden box with a lid on top. Underneath was a five-gallon bucket. *Wow, this is nice,* I thought. *At least we don't have to sit in a little shack out back where the mosquitoes can feast on us.* But this was not the time to walk around and gawk. There was work to do—and people to meet. I do declare, if there were a hundred people in the village, every single one came to our house. And why not? After all, this was the land where the natives had lived for generations. I would gradually begin the process of learning that we, the white man, were the foreigners.

The people were friendly, helpful, and eager to know our names. The children were especially outgoing—no trace of shyness there! Eventually the plane was unloaded, and Leonard showed us a few things about the house, one of which was how to carry a bucket of water from the lake to the house.

"But Leonard, you don't mean all our water has to be carried up the hill from the lake, do you?" I queried.

"Oh, there is a choice. You are welcome to take your baths in the lake."

"Yeah, right," I muttered.

Leonard revved the engine of the Pilatus, skimmed across the water, and was soon airborne. We watched him disappear in the west.

Suddenly our little family realized that we were now alone, on a native reserve called Slate Falls in northwestern Ontario. No, we were not alone, not by a long shot. But we realized that we did not know one single person in the area. Neither could we go somewhere to visit family. We realized that we couldn't just go and call a driver to take us somewhere to go shopping. Although we were told there was a telephone somewhere in the village, it was said to be difficult to connect a long-distance call.

We were hungry, so Edna found some food and we were soon sitting around the table in our house—our home. We would soon find out what life was like in the far north.

As we ate our lunch, we were entertained by little faces peering through every window. Other children stood inside the door, watching curiously while we ate our lunch.

The first afternoon we were busy unpacking our things and discovering interesting little shacks on the property. There was even a little log cabin where I could have a shop. Attached to the far side of the cabin was a lean-to that we could use for a church.

Chapter 6

Getting Settled

Many people stopped in to say *"Bosho."*[1] The trouble was, they all looked the same! It was kind of embarrassing when we asked the same people the same questions. The people were friendly, but not exactly talkative. Of course, there were exceptions. Charlotte and Liz, two of the natives, told us everything about everyone. Charlotte soon shared that she was the only native Christian in the whole community. Liz was considered the mayor of Slate Falls.

We also got acquainted with Jim and Mary Keesic. Jimmy was a native from Red Lake who married Mary Miller, a worker for the mission. She was from Wayne County, Ohio, not far from our Ohio

---

[1] "Hello" in the native language.

home. Jimmy was a Christian and had graduated from college with a teaching degree. Now he was in Slate Falls as a schoolteacher. It was indeed a welcome feeling to have Jimmy and Mary and their three children living almost next door. Mary could even speak our native language, Pennsylvania Dutch.

After most of the welcoming committee had left, we decided to take a walk down the little trails through the bush. There were many swampy areas. One of the first things we had noticed when we landed was that everyone, both young and old, was wearing boots. Now we knew why. They were a must to navigate these muddy trails.

One of the first houses we came to was where Charlotte lived with her husband Levius. Charlotte told us that Levius sometimes gets drunk. We moseyed on and soon found Dinah's house, where she lived with her two children, Don and Kathy. Dinah was very friendly but spoke very little English, so we soon passed on to the next house, where Liz lived. She was eager to show off her six children. Liz then went with us to the next few houses.

We stopped to say *bosho* to Flora and her sister Candy. Next we stopped briefly at Gilbert's house. Gilbert was the "gas man." He was an entrepreneur who purchased fifty-gallon drums of gas and had it flown in. He would then sell it to people in the community for a profit. Flora, Candy, and Gilbert were all siblings. Farther up the trail lived their uncle Philip. Philip was an older man who insisted on doing everything the old way. He was skilled in making snowshoes and boat paddles. He had never learned more than a handful of English words.

We had now completed our tour of the "Loon" end of the community, named for a family whose last name was Loon. All the homes were built with logs. They were one-room structures with plywood for the walls, sealed off with roll roofing. I secretly wondered how they could keep them warm in the winter. We were already overwhelmed with the mosquito population and were beginning to understand the local saying: "Mosquitoes are never single. They are all married with large families."

After coming back from our mini tour, we felt like we knew a little more about our surroundings. We were encouraged by the friendliness of the people. But we were also experiencing a bit of culture shock. Our Amish culture is simple, so we had expected some changes. But we were taken aback by some of the things we encountered, especially the long hair of some of the men. A few had ponytails reaching down to their waist. Most of the younger teenage girls wore trousers with bell-bottom flares that they had skillfully altered by inserting a V-shaped cloth of various colors. Pink seemed to be their favorite.

We decided to have a snack and then go to the other end of the village, where we hoped to find the telephone. Starting off, we came to a wooden boardwalk. Apparently the swamp had been so deep that it was necessary to bridge it with walkways. The first house we came to was the teacherage where Jim and Mary Keesic lived. Their house had been built in sections during various times when the need for another room arose. An older couple, Tom and Emily Carpenter, occupied the next house. They turned out to be a very interesting couple. Tom was a terrific storyteller and had many tales to tell.

Next we came to the schoolhouse. Built of logs, it was only several years old. The more I saw of the community, the more intrigued I became of this remote little village. Although most of the people were friendly, others were quite shy, hiding behind their long black hair.

Living in Slate Falls is going to be a cakewalk, I decided. From the very start, I had imagined it would be romantic and intriguing—maybe almost like being semi-retired. I looked back at my wife and three children who were following me single file along the narrow trail. "This is absolutely great!" I said. "We will love living here." I should know. After all, we had lived here nearly a whole day. Edna almost nodded her head, but I wasn't sure. *She just needs a good night's rest,* I thought.

We soon arrived in a little clearing with two houses that seemed to be quite populated. We wondered if maybe this was where we would find the phone. We couldn't wait to call home and tell our family what a great place Slate Falls was. The door to one of the houses was open, so we walked in and looked around for a pay phone. Not finding one, we inquired and were told it was in the next room. The phone was, in fact, in one of the local's living room. His name was Sam.

The telephone company, Bell Canada, was required by the Canadian government to provide phone service to all of the northern reserves, this being part of a complicated treaty between the whites and the natives. The treaty addressed many issues, including health care. This treaty has always been a point of contention. Our goal was to remain neutral.

We soon learned that Sam was an elder in the community. In order to provide phone service, there needed to be electricity, so Bell Canada installed a generator powered by a diesel engine. As payment to Sam for providing a shelter for the phone, Sam's house had the luxury of electricity.

The room was a bit on the dark side, but we could see at least six people sitting in the room. They acknowledged our *bosho* but didn't volunteer more.

"We came to see if we could use your phone, sir," I began.

Sam spoke up. "You don't have to ask. Just come in and use it!"

The phone sat in the corner of Sam's living room, but it had no dial or keyboard. We looked at it, puzzled.

"Just lift the receiver and wait for an operator," someone in the room instructed. "When an operator answers, tell them you are calling from Slate Falls. They will ask what number you wish to call."

We followed the instructions and were finally able to connect with the home folks and tell them we had arrived safely and what a beautiful place it was. We didn't visit very long until someone poked a head around the corner and asked, "How long will you be on the phone?" We wanted to be accommodating, so our first phone call was very short. We visited briefly with the family who lived in the house, then headed back up the trail the way we had come. Along the way we met more new people—or at least we thought they were new.

It so happened that we had made our journey north when the days were the longest. When we got back to our house, it was 9:30 but barely starting to get dark. We heard children yelling and laughing behind the house and discovered there was a volleyball court back in the bush.

By 10:30, the day was finally beginning to come to an end. We watched as the last rays of the sun disappeared behind the forest at the western end of the lake. It was truly breathtaking. The community was finally settling down for a short summer night—and so was the Troyer family.

We walked down to the lake and sat on the edge of the dock, our

Getting Settled

feet dangling in the water as we listened to the night noises around us. Almost in any direction, we could hear the occasional barking of a dog. At times we heard the splashing of a fish or some other water animal. From far across the lake came the drone of an outboard. Apparently a fisherman was out late for an evening catch.

The only problem with the peaceful summer evening was the constant drone of hordes of mosquitoes, all there to welcome us to Slate Falls. It was late when we got to bed, and oh, were we tired. The mattress we slept on left much to be desired, but we were tired enough to sleep anyway.

Adjusting to Life in the Bush

I woke up and looked at the clock. *What's going on?* I wondered. The clock showed 4:30, but sunlight was streaming in through the bedroom window. We knew then that we must put some blinds on our bedroom windows, and black garbage bags proved to be just the thing. I had planned to have good, long nights of rest. But with the sun shining nineteen hours a day, and people coming and going until late at night, this didn't seem to fit my expectations.

Our second day at Slate Falls found us exploring the little shacks around the house and going for a boat ride, which was something we had no experience with as I never did care much for fishing. I liked eating fish and enjoyed riding in a boat, but fishing was not my sport. After trying everything we could think of, we finally got our outboard going and headed off in the direction that seemed logical. Suddenly we hit some rocks. We knew this was not good. The sooner you learn where the rocks are, the sooner the natives accept you.

What we were not told, and what we did not guess, was that there were huge rocks all over the lakes, many of them only a foot under the water. We could not see them, but it seemed they were clearly out to snag hapless boaters like us. The natives knew where every single rock was for miles around. I resolved to learn their whereabouts as well. I eventually did learn the dwelling place of most of them—after several years of hitting them.

It did not take long to discover that to hit a rock with a boat was as close to the bottom of the "Totem Pole of Prestige" as I would find myself for some time. Little did we know how many eyes were peeping from the bushes along the shoreline, now fully persuaded that the Troyer tribe was just like the rest of the white people: not created for the bush!

Another thing we had to figure out was how to use the old wood stove in the kitchen. When we first entered the house and saw the Home Comfort wood stove, I thought it was quite decorative for this pioneer setting, little realizing how much we would use it. It was what my wife would use for all our cooking and baking needs.

We found some dry wood in an old shack behind the house and soon had the old wood stove shedding a respectable amount of heat. When we deemed it hot enough, we carefully put in the pans laden with their doughy material. The product that emerged twenty minutes later could well have been a soot-covered rock, but after peeling off about three layers, we found what we were looking for—soft, doughy bread. It did not take long for Edna to learn the skill of firing the stove. Get it hot, cool it back down, then insert the bread. Some of the best bread I have ever eaten came from the old Home

Comfort wood stove.

Days came and went, most of them very quickly. Every day we learned new things. Little by little we discovered that the people did not all look the same, and they had names just like we did. Oh, there were no Troyers, Schlabachs, Yoders, Millers, or Rabers, but there were Carpenters, Wesleys, Roundheads, Bigheads, Shakakeesics, Loons, Masakayashs, and more. Many of them knew only a few English words, but some spoke it very well. Usually we were not far from someone who was able and willing to be our translator. There was never a shortage of people willing to give free advice—whether we needed it or not.

One morning as I stepped outside the door I looked across the lake, which was only fifty feet from our front door. The sun was just showing its glow on the eastern horizon. The lake was as smooth as glass. Far across the bay I heard the lilting cry of a common loon. Moments later a mate answered from behind the point. Life couldn't be much better than this! Then I heard the soft hum of an outboard coming across the lake. It appeared to be barely moving. Eventually I was able to determine that it was a boat powered by a small outboard motor pulling a huge raft of logs and coming in my direction.

The man on board soon tied his raft to a tree along the shore and slowly came my way. He greeted me with a friendly *bosho* and introduced himself as Ivan Cook. With a few words, he asked if I would cut the logs on the sawmill. He said he was building a house across the lake on an island, pointing with his lower lip in that direction. In my earlier explorations around our home, I had discovered an old sawmill partially hidden in the grass next to the forest. It didn't look like anything that would work anymore, and I had no idea how to operate it even if it did. We walked to the mill, and as I took a closer look, I found an old four-cylinder Wisconsin engine that looked like it had gone through either the Great Flood or the Great Depression. My new friend assured me that it still worked.

I helped Ivan pull his logs onto the shore and then went inside for a late breakfast. I explained to my family that I had my work cut out for a while, resetting the old sawmill on solid timbers and trying to get the old Wisconsin running. I had always hated those old die-hards. They never ran nicely, but they never completely gave up the ghost either. I was always convinced that Wisconsin engines were built with a brain that could sense exactly when their operator had had just enough of cranking, backfiring, and kicking, and then suddenly, without any ceremony, they'd begin to run. This one played its role quite well!

The sawmill was equipped with a crank on a chain to pull the carriage laden with a log through a dangerous-looking blade that wobbled and sang various tunes, depending on its speed and other factors. I did my best to convince Ivan that I knew all about sawmills and Wisconsin engines. The timbers on which this sawmill was mounted were very much in need of replacement, so I decided to do that first. After all, this is what my dad always tried to impress upon me: "Anything worth doing is worth doing right."

I selected two long, straight trees in the forest nearby, which I then cut and used for the foundation of the sawmill. Eventually, after several days of work, I had the old sawmill set up and the Wisconsin purring like a kitten. Well, almost.

I went in search of Ivan and told him we could start to cut his logs the next morning. At the appointed time, Ivan arrived at the sawmill.

After a half dozen belches and groans, the old Wisconsin roared to life and seemed to enjoy its job. The work went surprisingly well, and by lunchtime we had a respectable stack of nice spruce boards. I loved the realization that we could cut trees from the hundreds of miles of forests, bring them to our crude sawmill, and cut them into nice boards. I eventually learned how to sharpen the blade to make a nearly perfect cut. Over the years, I took great pleasure in seeing the natives bring rafts of logs to the sawmill for cutting.

Ivan was a hardworking man, built like a weightlifter. I always said that anything two other men could lift onto their shoulders, Ivan could carry by himself. We had no equipment to haul logs out of the bush, so we helped each other get this job done. If we had three men, Ivan being one of them, logging was fairly easy.

There were other methods to do our logging. One method I used quite a bit required two men, a boat, and about a hundred feet of strong nylon rope. One man would fell the trees, trying to throw them toward the shore. He would trim the limbs, then use the nylon rope to tie the log to the boat. The second man would back the boat close to the shore and give the outboard motor full throttle. The momentum would move the log a little closer to the shore. The boat driver would keep doing this until the log was in the water.

Perhaps the hardest part in using this method was to corral the logs. The most common way was to wade out into the water, tie the logs together in the shape of a large circle, then lead the rest of the logs into this circle.

Understandably, this method required absolutely quiet waters. If there were even small waves, the logs in the corral would bounce up and down and soon find their way to areas that weren't part of the plan. This was why we did this work early in the morning.

One morning I had a big boom of logs ready to sail early. I left our house before daylight, hooked my boat to the boom, and gradually got it moving. Once it started to move, it did not take much power to keep it moving. The sun was coming up and the loons were calling to each other. It was a great morning to be alive. It was going very well. I stood up in my boat and was singing at the top of my voice. All of a sudden I hit a reef, and try as I might, the logs would not float over the top of it. Let's just say that once you get six cords of wood stranded, you have a problem. That's why my singing came to an abrupt halt.

The way the natives love to tell this story is something like this: "Early one morning someone was singing loudly out on the lake. It sounded nice. Then, *Bang! Bang!* And the singing stopped. I looked out the window and there was Edwin standing in his boat looking around trying to figure out how to get his raft off that reef. Even as he stood there, a few of the logs were sneaking out from under him."

I gladly sacrificed my pride for the fun of having something for the natives to laugh about. I suppose they are still laughing at me to this day.

We all had to make adjustments—some more of a challenge or more comical than others. But we all worked hard to do what needed to be done. Sometimes people from the States asked, "Do you have running water?" The answer was, "Yes, if you fill a bucket with water and run!" We were beginning to feel quite comfortable with life in the bush, which included carrying all our water in buckets that we dipped from the lake. What we didn't enjoy—and even dreaded—was carrying the "wastes" in the five-gallon bucket out to the bush.

Edna got the Home Comfort cook stove trained quite well, and we heated all our water on it. This was a bit of a challenge because the stove could get quite warm. We found a large galvanized tub that worked perfectly. We would fill the tub with water, fire up the stove in the morning, and enjoy having warm water all day. It felt like a luxury.

Eventually we got used to not going to bed early—eleven o'clock was early. We learned and memorized the trails and boardwalks throughout the community. Our children adjusted to going to school where all kinds of shenanigans took place. The bigger boys might have a knife-throwing contest during class. If you walked into the classroom, you would never guess that school was in session.

We soon got used to wearing boots most of the time, just as everybody else did. The boots that were most popular were black with red soles. With some practice, the younger children learned how to roll the top of the boot down one round. Our children thought it was pretty "cool." The students were required to remove their shoes or boots when in class. It's not hard to imagine the smell of thirty to forty children removing their sweaty feet from those rubber boots.

Every day brought new adventures. Slowly but surely we were learning to adjust to this new life in the bush.

Chapter 7

The Violent Party

One morning in the fall of 1981, I followed my normal morning procedure of waking up, stepping outside on the little open porch attached to our house, and taking a deep breath of the exhilarating northern air. The mornings and evenings were already much closer together. This was September, with chilly mornings and misty pockets of fog scattered here and there across the lakes. A serene, almost sacred, hush enveloped the little village of Slate Falls.

We had lived here for nearly five months and felt quite well adjusted. Our contacts with the people had not brought about any life-changing experiences, but we hoped that would come. We knew we first needed to build relationships and then have faith that the rest would follow. In spite of feeling comfortable and relaxed that morning, something seemed to tell me, "Things aren't going to always be like this." It felt like Satan was arranging the stage for his turn at demonstrating his tactics.

Across the lake from our house was an island with a half-finished log cabin, as well as an open cook tent and three other tents. We somewhat knew these people, because occasionally some of them showed up for church services. We had also been on the island several times. The children, however, were the ones we knew best. It seemed the parents enjoyed the privilege of bringing them across the lake to the mission house to play with our children for the day. Two girls nearly the age of our girls were on our shoreline more than they were on their own. Usually they showed up around 2:00 in the afternoon. Sometimes they even spent the night with our girls.

On this particular day, the girls had arrived early and were acting a bit strange. They would come into the house, then go back outside and hide in the bushes, often peering across the lake to their tent homes.

Finally we were curious enough to ask, "Girls, is something wrong over on your island?"

"They are drinking over there," they replied. "We're scared!"

We had heard of wild drinking parties in the reserves, but so far we had not had a problem and were not overly alarmed. We assured the girls that they were safe here at the mission house and were welcome to stay overnight if they wished. This was an obvious consolation to them. Now we also started keeping an eye on the island.

By around 6:00, the sun began casting long, dark shadows across the forests and lakes of Slate Falls. But unseen to our eyes were the dark shadows Satan was casting upon the little island across the lake from us. As the darkness increased, the shouts and screams on the island increased, and it was obvious why our young friends wanted to stay at our house.

As time went on, a boatload of older people came to our dock. With a combination of a few English words and their native Ojibwa, they got the message across. "They are drinking. Fighting real bad. We come to mission house. Sleep here maybe?"

"Yes, you may stay here," was our reply. We didn't realize there would be more people coming for refuge as the night developed.

At one point, a boatload of "drinkers" came to our dock, cursing and swearing and fighting. One fellow who was drunk was in the water up to his knees. The bad part was that he was in headfirst! We were not too happy to have the "drinking group" around our premises, but asking them to leave only cemented their determination to stay and break into our house.

By now it was midnight. Our house was full of people, young and old, who had come to our house for refuge. I decided to leave my guard duty at the front door long enough to go through our house to take inventory of who really was present. We had turned off all the lights to discourage the cursing, fighting mob that was trying to come in.

Little by little I sensed my own attitude changing. It went from casual understanding to disgust to downright anger. We had come to help these people—now they act like this! At this dark hour, when I felt responsible to have my children all safely and peacefully in bed, I cautiously stepped through my house. It was "wall to wall" with people. And outside, the fighting, cursing, and swearing continued. Occasionally the house shook from the impact of someone being thrown against it. I wondered when a rock might come through a window.

Around 1:00 the mob started to calm down a bit—but the mob within me had just begun. Through the darkness and shadows, the house looked like a war zone of bodies. I didn't have any idea where my wife and children were.

As I surveyed the scene, I heard someone crying out. From the island across the lake, I heard a voice screaming, "Mama! Mama!" I recognized the voice. These people had been to church a few times.

At this moment, at the darkest hour of the night, and probably the darkest hour of my missionary endeavors, I decided this was hopeless. As my disgust approached a near rage at these people whom we had come to evangelize, I decided that the next day we would make arrangements to move back to Sugarcreek, Ohio. There, the people all knew each other, understood each other, and for the most part, loved each other. This was not the place for us.

I took one last stroll around the outside of the house. Most of the drinkers had disappeared, but a few were still lying here and there. I cautiously went upstairs, wondering if my wife would be there. I wasn't sure if it was worth crawling into bed or not; it would be morning in a couple hours.

I was an angry and bitter man, something no missionary should be. I finally fell asleep with that haunted cry of our friend echoing in my ears—"Mama! Mama!"

A Vision and a Mandate

I woke with a start. Had all this drinking and partying driven me crazy? In a dream, I had seen things I had never seen before, and I had heard a voice speaking to me. Quietly I lay in bed, thinking. Yes, my mind was still functioning. I tried to put the scenes together. Did I have a dream? Or was it a vision? As I tried to review and analyze what I had seen and heard, I decided it didn't matter what I named it. It was a message from God. And it was for me, Edwin Troyer.

In my dream/vision, I was standing on the shores of Bamadji Lake, the lake in front of our house. Only the lake did not contain the clear blue water as usual. Instead, the water looked like used motor oil. The whole lake was full of it. Not only that, but it was on fire. And instead of the flames lighting up the area, they seemed to make the darkness more intense. In spite of the darkness, I could see clearly. As far as I could see, there were tongues of fire and smoke.

The oily waves were perhaps two feet high. Then I realized that there were people swimming in the oily, burning lake. As I looked closer, I began to recognize the people who were swimming and struggling in this lake of burning oil. I heard them calling out, "Help! Help!" Suddenly I was aware that this was the "Lake of Fire" that we read of in the Revelation. Looking deeper into the darkness, I could see an endless stream of people struggling, swimming, trying to stay on top. All were screaming, "Help us! Help us!"

Then I heard it—or maybe it would be more accurate to say I felt it—a deep, enveloping Voice saying, "You must tell these people what you are seeing."

My answer was, "God, I can't. I don't love them anymore." My mind was made up. The next day I would make preparations to move back to Ohio, a land where people lived predictably. Oh sure, there were people who sometimes acted in ways they shouldn't. But it was nothing like this.

My mind snapped back to reality when I heard the Voice again. "You weren't very lovable either, but I still gave my life for you."

I realized God had given me a mandate to minister to these needy people. I sealed the contract with God by promising, "Yes, God, I will."

The remainder of the night was without incident. There were still people scattered all through the house, sleeping wherever they could find a spot, and there were still a few drunken people lying on the grass outside our house. But I now saw them in a totally different light. I saw them as real people with real souls who were headed for a real lake of fire, which I had just seen.

I went to bed and actually fell asleep, but soon the sun was rising for another day. People started to wake up in our house. My wife began cooking breakfast for all who wished to eat. After a while, when all our uninvited sleepers were gone, I got my family together for our time of devotions. We all had much to share, but the vision God had given me certainly caught my family's attention, and we all determined to be more serious about our purpose of being here at Slate Falls. Were we here to have a good time? Must things always go well? No, life is not that way.

We tried our best to act normal and go about our duties that day. For the most part, those involved in the party did not show their faces—except one. The young woman was shy, but she managed to say, "I am sorry for what happened last night." We assured her that we were also sorry.

After a few days, everything seemed fairly normal again. I wondered when I'd have the opportunity to speak to the participants of that awful party. I wondered when I could fulfill the mandate God had so dramatically given me. Was there a perfect time for something like this? The next Sunday morning, I purposed to make the trip across the lake that afternoon. It was so close and yet so far. I dreaded to go, but I knew I must. After church was over, we ate a light lunch, and I knew the time had come. I had to go tell them what God had told me.

Fulfilling My Promise

I launched our boat into the clear blue water of Bamadji Lake, no longer a lake of fire. As I approached the little island, I noticed a number of people working on something. I hesitated. "God, this is not a good time. Can I do it another time?"

His answer seemed clear: "Now is the time." I tied my boat and very slowly walked up the trail to where the people were gathered. I quickly observed that these were all people who had been involved in the drinking party. Now they were busy butchering a moose someone had shot. They seemed not to notice that I was there. Nobody said a word, even though I made a futile attempt at small talk.

Finally I cleared my throat. "I am here to . . . ah . . ." I began. "I am here to tell you . . . ah . . . that God wants me to tell you . . .

ah . . . something." I managed to blurt out the whole story rather quickly. They kept on cutting meat, not saying a word. All was silent.

In fact, from the moment I arrived, nobody had said a word. I thanked them for their time and slowly walked the winding footpath back to the boat.

When I was halfway there, one of them said, "Thank you, Edwin. Nobody ever told us anything like that."

I wondered why God had not given me a gift of speaking with at least a little bit of eloquence for just those few minutes. "Dear God," I prayed, "I am sorry I failed so miserably. I really did try."

Chapter 8

"Can You Help Me?"

As fall approached, the days began getting shorter. By now, our acquaintance with the natives was such that they freely came to our house to visit. From early morning till late at night, it seemed there were always people at the mission house. There were two ladies who believed it was their duty and God-given talent to report all the latest news or "gossip." Some of this was legitimate news, but most of it would have been better left in the bush somewhere.

All was silent from the folks on the island to whom I had testified of my dream. Occasionally a few of them came to church, which was really encouraging. I hoped maybe my speech was more helpful than I had thought. One Sunday evening more people attended than usual, and among them was Canasia, the lady who had given that lonely cry at 1:00 in the morning. She seemed to hang around the entrance to the church, so I made my way to where she was standing. I tried to have a conversation, but she seemed not to hear what I was saying. I was slowly learning that the natives do not need to talk to visit. So I just stood there and "listened" to her not saying anything. Finally she took a deep breath and asked, "Edwin, would you come over tomorrow? I need to talk to somebody."

"Yes," I told her. "I'll be over in the morning." I couldn't wait to tell my family about her request.

The next morning Edna and I pointed our boat to the little island where Canasia lived with Sam Cook. Once we arrived, we tied our boat and made our way to the log cabin. I knocked on the battered, wooden door. A small blue rope was ingeniously wrapped around a nail to serve as a latch. I knocked again but heard nothing. I wondered if Canasia had forgotten that she had asked me to come. I knocked again. This time I heard a low mumble from inside. I assumed somebody was inviting me to come in. The door opened with a squeak as it scraped across the floor.

I looked around the dark little cabin with only two windows. As my eyes adjusted to the darkness, I was able to take inventory of what was inside. On the far wall, there appeared to be a bedroom with an old blanket slung over the entrance for privacy.

The wall to my left then came into focus. This was the "kitchen." I wondered what my wife would say if that was all she had for a kitchen. A large bowl hung from a nail, and several smaller utensils hung here and there. A little table was crudely nailed together with an old piece of plywood. It looked as if it had spent most of its life in the forest somewhere.

I finally realized that the woman who had invited us was sitting on a chunk of firewood in the corner to my left. Canasia sat with her face in her hands. Her elbows rested on her knees, and her long black hair hung over her face. I made my presence known with small talk, but she seemed not to hear. So I found another block of firewood and sat upon it. Once I had given up the white man's method of talking to visit, I realized she was crying.

After another ten minutes of "visiting," Canasia sat up, pushed her hair to the back of her head, and revealed her face. It was obvious that she had been crying for some time. Between sobs, she finally managed to tell me that ever since that time when I had told them about the vision, she could not sleep or eat. "I am a sick woman," she said. "I know I am going to hell."

I wondered how to explain the plan of salvation to a person who did not grow up in a Christian setting. We can make it sound easy, or we can make it sound hard. I opened my Bible and read some Scriptures that I hoped would explain how a person can come to Christ. Canasia looked at me through bleary eyes and said, "But you don't know what a wicked person I am."

In the next hour, we learned more about this weary woman than we could have imagined. She confessed to us that Sam, the man she was living with, was not her husband. In fact, she had had many husbands—and many children.

Canasia was very open and just poured out her life story. She knew it was not right for her to live with Sam anymore. As we considered what the Bible has to say about divorce and remarriage, the options were few. She knew she must part from her common-law relationship and was willing to give it a try. She knew Sam would not understand, and she worried about her girls. They loved their daddy. We had prayer, and then slowly got to our feet to go home. I was both happy and sad as we headed back to our house.

As we relayed the happenings of our visit to the rest of the family, we started to realize how complicated this could become if Canasia wanted to be truly Scriptural. She had children who needed a mother and father. She would need a place to live. She would need some income to buy food. And likely nobody would understand such radical behavior. The following week provided very little interaction with her. We wondered what she would do. Would she follow through with her commitment, or would she decide that being a Christian was too hard?

A week later she came to visit and told us that Sam wanted to go to his trapline cabin on Keesic Lake and had asked her to go along. It was typical for families to have a small cabin on their trapping area. This way they could bring their family for two or three months and do their trapping. Hopefully they could harvest a moose or two, or a caribou, and enjoy being together in the great outdoors. This was a traditional venture that I had always encouraged. But now I wondered if this was the right thing for Canasia, a new convert, to be in such a living arrangement.

We had not encountered this kind of situation before. We made a few phone calls to ministers and friends asking for prayer and wisdom. Canasia and her children were now gone from the village, and we were not exactly sure where they were. All we knew was that they were somewhere in an old trapper's shack with no means of communication, so we were somewhat able to lay aside some of our thoughts and concerns. In the meantime, many prayers went forth for her.

Weeks passed and we heard nothing from Canasia. Summer gradually shifted into fall. The leaves on the deciduous trees showed off their bright red and yellow hues. Our early morning peeks out of our bedroom windows revealed frost on the grass. The days were now much shorter. Our neighbors kept telling us how cold the weather would get in the winter. There were stories of soft spots in the ice where people would break through and drown or just simply freeze in the minus-sixty-degree weather. There were times when we were apprehensive about the coming of winter.

We knew it would take lots of firewood to keep us from the fate that some of the natives seemed to enjoy sharing about the "greenhorn white people" from down south. But when I'd talk to the natives about firewood, they would say, "You don't need to worry about firewood until it gets cold and you need it!" I didn't agree. I was going to be prepared. I wanted to be sure we had enough firewood piled against our house to keep us warm all winter.

Someone from the mission in Red Lake said there was supposed to be firewood somewhere that belonged to us, but they had no idea where it might be. I asked my friend Ivan if he knew anything about firewood belonging to us, and he pointed across the lake with his lower lip. I decided that the next day I would find that woodpile. I knew that might be a challenge because Ivan's lip seemed to point everywhere. The next morning I took our boat and headed in the general direction Ivan had pointed. After searching for several hours on little islands, I found piles of wood cut to four-foot lengths and neatly piled. I assumed this must be our firewood. I decided to head back home and figure out a way to transport the firewood across the lake.

As I got closer to our dock, I noticed an unfamiliar boat tied there. By now we were able to recognize every boat in the community. As I docked my boat and started up the boardwalk to our house, I met a young fellow I had never seen before. He was friendly and we visited awhile, then he reached into his pocket and pulled out a crumpled piece of paper, handing it to me. "I was coming past Keesic Lake when I saw Sam and Canasia and their two girls at their cabin. When Canasia heard that I am on my way to Slate Falls, she asked if I could deliver a message to you."

As soon as I read that crumpled little paper, the tremendous responsibility of mentoring a newborn babe in Christ immediately hit me. I had very strange emotions. We had traveled all these miles with the purpose of teaching these people who were not raised the way we were, people who had possibly never heard sound doctrine. This was what we came for, to bring people to a saving knowledge of Jesus Christ. But lately we had felt so relaxed to just live here in Slate Falls.

We were having church services every Sunday morning and evening in the small lean-to beside our shop. We had also started having a Bible study on Wednesday evening. Even though a program like this entailed a fair amount of studying, it was not a high-tension responsibility. In fact, it was starting to feel comfortable.

The crumpled piece of paper from this messenger's pocket read, "Edwin and Edna, I have been thinking about how I am living. I want to come to Slate Falls. I will also bring my daughters. Can you share your home so you can teach me the way of Jesus?"

Canasia's note went on to say that she had no money, no beds, no pots and pans, and no food. She said she thought she had a way to travel to Slate Falls the next week.

I shared the scribbled note with my family. I was impressed that they seemed more enthusiastic than I was. After all, this would change our relaxed schedule completely. To have three new people in our household would bring to light the little family differences we had from time to time. But we soon realized we had no choice. We came here to lead people to the Lord. What would Jesus do? Would He tell them to go somewhere else because our house is full? I doubted it.

The next few days were busy ones. We agreed that Canasia and her girls could stay in the one room upstairs. They could join our devotions each morning, and they would eat from our table. We were willing to give it a try. The following Thursday, Sam Cook's boat showed up at our dock loaded with many bags and cardboard boxes, which they began to unload. Sam did not look one bit happy. He had not known anything about the change in Canasia's life. He spoke not one word to me, and I realized this was not easy for him. Sam was not a Christian, so it made no sense to him. He and Canasia had been together for thirteen years, had two children together, and loved each other. Now here we come and convince his partner to leave him. Yes, I could understand why he felt this way.

We as a family had to put on our best face. Having strangers living with us in our little house brought added responsibility in our daily living. I constantly had to remind myself that this was what we were there for.

After Canasia and the girls were settled in their room, our family discussed the situation. A few of us were happy for the challenge, but we all wondered why Canasia was so somber, so withdrawn. We soon realized that the change was even greater for her and her daughters than it was for us. These people had lived most of their lives in tents in the bush. They were used to sleeping on a thin foam pad and sitting on chunks of firewood for their chairs. To live in a white man's house was depressing for them. A week passed rather quickly, but not without some challenges. Yes, they tried to appear happy, but we could tell that they felt like fish out of water.

Then one day Edna came up with an idea. "Why don't we clear out the log cabin shop, fix it up a bit, and move them in there?" We suggested this to Canasia, and she was excited about the idea. Within a week we had the old shop looking almost attractive. We had patched some cracks and holes, made several crude bedframes, and found a few mattresses. A barrel was adapted for use as a wood stove.

Canasia and her daughters were as excited to move into the cabin as we were to have our privacy back. Canasia's whole personality changed. Sure, she was at our house a lot, but now she felt much more at home in her own setting. She eagerly studied her Bible and wrote down any questions she had. Almost every day we would go through her questions and try to answer them. We enjoyed the times we spent together with Canasia studying the Bible. We felt totally at ease with her. We were thrilled that she was happy in her new home and seemed settled and growing in her Christian life.

From Foe to Friend

If you are wondering what happened to Sam Cook, I have a story for you.

After Canasia and her daughters moved in with us, we put quite a bit of effort into befriending Sam, hoping he could understand why there were so many changes in Canasia. He was an angry man, especially toward us. It seemed that every attempt we made to reconcile our friendship failed. He didn't understand why his wife would not come home or why things couldn't be like they were before. At times we would take food to Sam's little cabin, but he refused anything we offered.

But then things did change—Sam Cook accepted the Lord! And oh, did that ever make a difference! Sam became one of my best friends. We even took him with us to the States one summer, and he helped on the farm. After a few years, Sam married a widow who was also a Christian, and they seemed to get along very well. As Sam got older, he had health issues that frequently landed him in the hospital. At this time we were back in Ohio, and one day I received a phone call from one of Sam's daughters, saying that her father was very sick and wanted to talk to me. Sam asked me to pray for him because he believed he was close to dying. I believe God listened in on our conversation. It was truly a touching moment. Sam could barely speak anymore and was breathing heavily. He was so grateful, however, and thanked me for my phone call and prayer.

Not long after this, we got another phone call from Sam's daughters to tell us that their dad had passed on into eternity. They said as he was dying, he kept saying something about how beautiful it is over there. They asked us to come to the funeral, which we did. The Gospel of Jesus Christ works. Sam Cook was living proof.

Chapter 9

Journey to Cat Lake

As a family, we were finally getting settled, but we were still concerned about the coming winter. We had heard so many stories of people getting stuck out on the lake with a snowmobile and then freezing to death, or breaking though the ice and drowning. Stories of hungry wolves attacking lone individuals also made us wonder if we were ready to face the giant of winter.

Like it or not, however, winter was coming, and I was kept busy making preparations. We devised a sled to hitch to our snowmobile, which we planned to use to haul the firewood that Ivan had pointed out to me. There was also a fair amount of firewood stacked near our house. I realized it would take lots of wood to heat not only our own house, but also Canasia's little cabin. I had finally figured out how to get our furnace working. It could be fed with five-foot logs and would easily hold fire for twelve hours. We were certainly thankful for that!

One morning in early November the thermometer showed minus five degrees, and we could see a thin layer of ice on the lake. The whole village was excited. Freeze-up at last! The sun shining on this wonderful white layer on the lake was beautiful beyond description. This created a whole new atmosphere in the community. Day after day the ice became thicker, and soon it was thick enough to support a snowmobile. I had never driven a snowmobile, much less serviced one in preparation to haul firewood.

Now that the ice was safe, the community's spirit changed. Whereas late October and November had been dreary, misty, cloudy, and sometimes depressing, the weather was now cold, sometimes twenty below zero, with lots of clear blue skies. A fresh new snow every few days reminded us of the Scripture about "our sins being whiter than snow."

I dug out the old snowmobile that belonged to the mission. It seemed to work okay, but what would I do if it didn't? I had never used one before. What I really wanted to do was go to Cat Lake by snowmobile. Cat Lake was our closest neighbor village, sixty-five miles to the north, as the crow flies. Some of the natives had made the trip and declared that the ice was good and strong. But for me, a white man who had never traveled the trail before, I wondered if I would be able to see the trail and follow it successfully. I asked a few of my friends what they thought.

Steven said, "I am telling you, Edwin, sixty-five miles through unmarked bush trails across forests and lakes is not an easy matter. You will get to places where the trail is snow-covered, and you will have no clue which way to go. Remember, the temperature will be thirty below zero. There are also hungry wolves out there. Why don't you wait until someone has time to go with you?"

When I asked Jake if it was smart for me to go to Cat Lake by myself, his reply was, "Why not? Just stay on the trail. Follow it and you'll be fine."

Edna listened to these conflicting voices of advice and finally decided, "Go ahead and make the trip. You will never be satisfied unless you try. We will pray for you."

As morning dawned on my chosen travel day, I was excited. I sorted through my collection of supplies I was gathering for the trip. My checklist was something like this: insulated coveralls, felt-lined boots, wool cap, muffler, warm wool mitts with long gauntlets, sunglasses, axe, rope, compass, enough food for a day, paper—in case it was necessary—and a small can of gas for the thirsty engine. I finally had everything stashed on the snowmobile.

I was dressed in nearly all the clothes I owned. Then, with the help of my wife and children, I forced my down-filled parka over the top of all my other layers. I felt like David dressed in Saul's armor, ready to fight Goliath. I wondered if I was also fighting a giant—a 130-mile trip through unmarked forests and lakes.

When the twin-cylinder snowmobile engine was warmed up and running smoothly, I slowly climbed on. I said goodbye to my family and headed north. Soon I was out of the village. I would never have confessed this, but I was bushed and this seemed like a way to get away from all the pressures of the reserve. I had not been out of the reserve in the six months we had been there. Now, as I traveled along all by myself in this winter paradise, I felt my mind unwinding. It was a wonderful feeling.

Occasionally my thoughts were interrupted by concerns of whether I was still on the right trail to Cat Lake. I soon discovered that it was a bit more complicated than Jake's advice to, "Just follow the trail!" You see, there were trappers out there checking their snares, and their tracks were all over the place. And they certainly weren't escorting Edwin Troyer on his maiden journey to Cat Lake! After considering the trails and the mind of a trapper, I picked out a well-packed trail, one that was a bit wider and seemed to be headed somewhere, not just making big circles, and followed it.

After I was again satisfied that I was on the right trail, I stopped the engine and just sat there in the wonderful winter paradise. Never in my life had I experienced such complete silence. The trees were mostly pine and spruce, along with some poplar and birch, but they all contributed to muffling any sounds. And what the trees did not do, the newly fallen snow did. It was so reverent, so beautiful, and so quiet. In spite of the temperature being twenty-four below, I had to take off my hat. I felt the presence of God in that place. After continuing my reverie and meditation for a while, I decided to continue my meditation while driving.

My mind went back to the time we had left Ohio eight months earlier and all that had transpired since then. We felt adjusted and enjoyed our new home, but sometimes the children had a day of homesickness. Overall, things were going well. Canasia and her two daughters were settled in and seemed happy, and there had recently been another convert in our community. Maxine, an older lady, had decided to follow Jesus. This brought joy to everyone. I marveled that even unbelievers were happy to hear of others who were bold enough to take that very important step.

My mind was so preoccupied with meditation and praise to God that I almost forgot where I was going or what I was doing, but the miles kept passing under the track of my trusty little snowmobile. I passed by several waterfalls, maybe more aptly called "rapids," but it was another demonstration of God's amazing beauty. In fast-flowing waters like this, the water did not freeze and kept on roaring down the river. As the mists and fog condensed in the treetops, it created a beautiful hoarfrost effect. I decided it was time for another meditation stop. I just wished I could have the opportunity to rename these rapids. On a map they were called the Devils Rapids.

I traveled on, realizing that the sun was casting more and longer shadows across the lakes. I knew that soon I should be getting to Cat Lake. Sure enough, across another lake and around a bend, there it was. I could faintly see the small houses with smoke rising from the chimneys.

I really did not know anyone in Cat Lake very well, only a few who had relatives living in Slate Falls. I had been assured that I would have a bed whenever we came to visit. Just the same, I was apprehensive. After all, most people did not know me, and Cat Lake was known as a rather rough place with lots of alcohol, suicides, fights, and occasionally even murders. After a prayer stop, I was ready to travel the remaining ten minutes to Cat Lake. The sun was setting, and I was cold but happy.

One of the first people I met when I drove into town was Pat Tepayook. He was very friendly and personable, and he immediately invited me to his house for the night. I was impressed. He gave me a quick rundown of who is who and where they live. He told me there were five hundred people living in Cat Lake, and they had a store called "The Northern." He said if I wanted to meet people, the store was the place to go because the natives bought only enough groceries to last a day. So to the store I went.

One of the first people I met at the store was Wilford, whom I had met before when he visited Slate Falls. He was a fierce-looking fellow—six-foot-plus, built like a giant, and sporting a big mustache. He greeted me in a booming voice that seemed to shake the building: "Well, here comes my personal rabbi!"

Most of the people I met were friendly and smiling. They wondered why I had come and how long I planned to stay. Before leaving the store, I bought a few items to make sure I wouldn't starve. But I needn't have worried!

My trip to Cat Lake was not just for adventure. I had hopes of starting a little Bible study group. The booklet I had was designed for readers to work one lesson a day. Then at the end of the week they would get together to discuss the lesson. I found a few interested people and made quite a few trips to Cat Lake to conduct the classes. It never really got going enthusiastically, but it gave us the opportunity to get to know the people, and years later it opened the door to other opportunities.

An Extended Stay in Cat Lake

Albert Wesley was a young man from Cat Lake whom we learned

to know. He was very assertive and outgoing, with lots of potential leadership abilities, but he lived a rough life. Because of his vices, and because his wife had been unfaithful to him, he was a miserable man. Albert eventually decided there was no point in living, so he decided to end his life. He was sure this would end the pain of the life he was living.

One morning, in the stillness and darkness before the break of dawn, he decided it was time to do it. Had it been possible to see the demons at work, we would have seen them rejoicing. Albert drove his snowmobile far out on the ice where he planned to do his evil deed. It was then that he noticed the first glow of sunrise. He had seen many sunrises in his life, but somehow this one was different. Everything was quiet. There were no motors, no lights, just total stillness. He was fascinated, full of reverence, as the eastern skies brightened. Then he realized it was Easter. He knew what had happened on Easter, but it had never meant anything to him.

God began working in Albert's heart as he sat there. In the silence of that Easter morning in the middle of a snow-covered lake, Albert decided to give God a chance. He bowed his head and acknowledged God through Jesus Christ. When the sun had fully risen, he drove slowly toward home, heading to the house where his wife was staying. He went to her bedside and begged her to forgive him. He promised to support her and accept her two children as his own, but she was not willing.

This was a beginning, but Albert had many more struggles.

As time went on, Albert was elected chief of the Cat Lake community. During his time in office, he contacted us, requesting that we come and live in Cat Lake for a few months. He explained that there were almost no Christians in Cat Lake. There were many murders and suicides, with much drug and alcohol abuse. Although it looked quite challenging to us, Edna and I decided to go to Cat Lake for three months, while our children kept the home fires burning.

This was in the dead of winter, and it was an adventure to get there. Albert's brother Wilford, whom I previously mentioned as a fierce-looking giant, met us at the small Cat Lake airport and drove us to a small house. We unloaded our gear on the doorstep, and Wilford drove off. We assumed this was an empty house, but when we tried to open the door, we found it locked—and from within a not-so-happy voice assured us that the house was indeed occupied.

A young lady opened the door. When we explained who we were, she said, "You can live here with me, but I'm not moving out!" We stepped inside and found it to be adequate, even though small. She showed us a room we could have for our bedroom. The bedroom had no door, and there was no plumbing and no toilet. After some discussion with the lady, whose name was Josie, we decided to give it a try. She said she was usually gone most of the day and came home late at night.

Living with Josie worked out quite well. She was single and very respectful of our beliefs. She came from a not-so-good home, and when we left a few months later, she told us, "You are more my parents than my real ones."

We tried to make the best of our living situation. Edna eventually collected enough utensils to create a semblance of a kitchen. As we took inventory of what Josie had, we noticed that most of the kitchen knives were burned black, and we wondered why. Later we found out that drug users often use knives to "cook" their habit by placing the drug on a knife and holding it over a lighter. It appeared living in Cat Lake was going to be a challenge.

Surprisingly, however, the next few months went well. We learned to know the people and found them quite friendly. We had access to an old log cabin that we used for church services and Sunday school. With Albert as chief, we were able to get the things we needed. There were times Albert would call me and ask if I would go for a walk with him—even if it was midnight and thirty degrees below zero. At first I wondered if this was necessary, but as we walked and he shared his innermost feelings, I realized that he really did need me.

When we headed back to Slate Falls, Albert invited us to come back the next winter. So for three more winters we went back to Cat Lake. Albert leaned heavily on us for emotional and mental support. Then, during the last winter we were there, Albert developed a bad cold, or so we thought. But it just would not respond to medication. After more examinations and tests, they discovered that Albert had cancer. We begged the Lord for healing, explaining to God that Albert was a potential leader, a Christian. "Why, Lord?"

After our last spring in Slate Falls, when we were on our way home to the States, we went to visit Albert. He was then living in Sioux Lookout so he could be close to the hospital. He looked very sick and frail. As I left his house, we hugged and he said, "Edwin, this is probably the last time I will see you on earth, but I will see you in heaven someday." The tears flowed. Approximately six weeks later I got the call that Albert Wesley had passed away the night before. I went to his funeral. It was in Cat Lake on Easter Sunday! How interesting that Albert found the Lord on Easter Sunday and three years later his funeral was also on Easter Sunday.

As mentioned earlier, Albert's brother Wilford was a dynamic person. He was always very accommodating to us, but he clung to some vices that made his life miserable. He had six children when his wife left him, the youngest only four weeks old. Several of them were raised by other family members. We often wondered if Wilford would ever accept Jesus and turn his life around.

Our hearts were thrilled during the winter of 2017 when I received a call from Wilford telling me that he had accepted the Lord. He requested that we send a missionary couple to Cat Lake to, as he said, "Show the people how to live."

Winter

Winter turned out to be our best ministry time. People were more cooped up and there was time to visit, play games, and read books. One of the more interesting activities was quilting. The ladies got together during the day and hand-sewed quilts, and in the evening the youth would show up and sit around the quilt while we read books to them. One book they really liked was *Light from Heaven* by Christmas Carol Kauffman. When it was time to quit for the day, the youth would beg, "No, you can't stop there. Read just one more chapter!"

Brazilian air force plane.

House in Brazilian Indian village.

View of Slate Falls in the 1980s.

Mission house where the Troyers lived during their first stay. The building on the right was Edwin's shop. The lean-to at the back was used for church services.

View out over the lake from a neighbor's house.

Jim and Mary Keesik and family.

Ivan Cook with the cupboards Edwin built for his new log house.

Canasia and her two daughters.

Sam Cook

Airplanes out on the ice.

Levius and Charlotte Wesley with their daughter-in-law and grandson.

106-year-old John Loon.

Edna and several pine grosbeaks. The birds came when she whistled, and were so tame that they picked out sunflower seeds from between her lips.

Edwin preparing to haul firewood.
It took about forty cords each winter.

The new church house the native people paid for.

Interior of the new church.

Chapter 10

Memorable People

One of our favorite things about living in Slate Falls and Cat Lake was the interesting people we met. They added so much color and joy to our lives, and they certainly made us laugh from time to time. As we slowly became acclimated to our new life there, they accepted us and became our friends. Some of these people were willing to hear us talk about our faith and beliefs. Others were not so willing. But that didn't stop us from trying.

As beautiful as this place was, there was also a harshness to some of the people. They lived hard, sometimes dark, lives. Many of them desperately needed God. Here are a few more stories from our time in the region.

Glenda

Glenda was a teenager. She was a beautiful young lady who appeared to have it all together. She lived in Cat Lake with relatives. Her parents had separated, and one year when we were having Bible school, Glenda spent a lot of time with Edna. She shared her inner struggles with many tears. "I want so much to be a Christian," she said. "But I just can't do it."

Time went on, and for several months we didn't hear much from her. One Sunday morning we got a call from her mother, telling us that they had found Glenda hanging in her bedroom. Suicide had been her solution to stop the pain. We traveled to Cat Lake, and her mother told us we could go into Glenda's room. Her frustrations were written on the four walls with an ink pen. It began on one wall, then became more intense on the next one. The words appeared to be a dialogue with someone. (It soon became clear that it was Satan.) On the last wall, written in large letters, Glenda words were, "Okay, I will do it!" We checked her player to see what music she had been listening to. It was a rock band of the most vulgar kind. Clearly, Glenda had yielded to the wrong voices. We were heartbroken that she didn't accept God's love for her and see the truth before it was too late.

Liz Bonnie

Liz Bonnie was not a Christian and had never shown any interest in church activities. One spring morning in 1994, Liz Bonnie was nowhere around. Search parties were soon organized, and planeloads of volunteers came from other reserves. For days, anyone who qualified was out searching. The volunteers slept in an empty cabin at night, and one night the searchers were awakened by some banging in the crawl space under the cabin. They were scared, but finally one of them had the nerve to open the crawl space and go in.

It was easy to see where the dirt had recently been disturbed, and here and there they saw drops of blood. It took a few minutes to build up enough courage to start digging. They soon found a dismembered arm, and then a leg. Before long, Liz Bonnie's complete body was uncovered. The searching continued, but now it was no longer for Liz—they were searching for her killer. Bloodhounds were brought in to assist in the search. The detectives acquired a coat that had been worn by Liz, and the dogs soon attacked a young man who was part of the search party. This happened to be Liz's boyfriend, Tony. With some more investigation, he was proved to be the killer.

We often wondered why Liz's boyfriend would choose to kill her. I can't imagine how that fellow felt with such guilt on his shoulders as he joined the search party for the young lady he had killed. And who was it that banged on the underside of the floor? The devil perhaps? I don't know. We may never have answers to some of these questions. This just showed us how far these people were from God.

Ellen

Ellen had a very strong personality. She also had many children. When we first met her, she had five of her older daughters with her.

She would share her frustrations as her daughters got older and more independent, saying they got into alcohol and drugs and everything that goes with that. She became frustrated with the lack of communication with her husband. He was quiet and shy, and whenever she talked to him, asking for help or advice, he would say nothing.

Edna spent many hours with Ellen, advising her to love her husband whether he responded or not. Then Ellen committed her life to the Lord, and she began to see significant improvements in her marriage. Her husband began responding in very positive ways. Ellen said he was becoming more thoughtful and loving toward her. Ellen is now a leader in the Cat Lake community, and she still calls us from time to time when she has struggles to work though.

Amelia

Amelia appeared in the community one spring day. To our surprise, we found out that she was Canasia's sister, though Canasia had never mentioned her. Amelia was married to a man named Isaac. They had quite a few children and lived out in the bush. Most of their married life was spent traveling from one trapper's cabin to another—fishing in the summer and trapping in the winter. But, sad to say, they had a real drinking problem.

When they arrived in Slate Falls, they had to live with someone, so they moved in with Canasia. We soon found out that Amelia was having health issues and needed medical attention. The doctor's diagnosis was not what they hoped to hear: Amelia had cancer—an advanced stage. One day Canasia told us that her sister knew almost nothing about the Bible. "Do you think you could talk to her, and I could interpret in Ojibwa?" she asked. The Indian language is a very difficult language and we never did master it. Our children did much better, picking it up in school.

As Canasia requested, we started trying to help Amelia. She was always very respectful and seemed to listen, but she was such a shy, quiet person, and we sometimes wondered how much she understood. But we kept on, trusting that God would speak to her. Months went by, and we could not see much change. In the meantime, Amelia's cancer was doing what cancer does so well, eating away on her body.

One day Amelia's niece Donna came to visit. Donna was a young lady who was fluent in English. She was not a Christian but had lots of Christian teaching, having boarded with a Mennonite family while going to high school. As Donna was ending her visit, Amelia said in a weak voice, "Donna, do you understand what the mission people are saying about the Bible and God and how to get to heaven? I understand some of what they say, but can you explain it to me in Ojibwa? I know you understand English very well."

Donna was a bit taken aback with such an awesome responsibility, but she finally found her voice. "Auntie, you must know that I am not a Christian." She cleared her throat. "But I think I know how to be one."

"Tell me, please." Amelia looked eagerly at her young niece. Donna realized the awesome responsibility that lay upon her. Donna knew the Bible, she knew the stories, and she knew the truth of the Gospel, but she had never been asked to explain these concepts to a dying person. Slowly Donna began to tell Amelia about Jesus. She told about His ministry, His death, and His resurrection. Once she got started, her assignment became easier. After an hour of speaking to her aunt, Donna felt free to leave, but she wondered if she had said the right things.

Donna soon appeared at the mission house, knocking on our door. We invited her in. Donna came in and sat down, but it was obvious she had something on her mind. She told us what she had done. Eagerly she leaned forward and asked, "Did I tell her right?" We felt she definitely had done so and assured her that God speaks all languages. We told her that the Holy Spirit would fill the gaps on anything she might have missed. We immediately sensed her great relief.

Time went on and we frequently stopped in to see Amelia. We would read a portion of Scripture to her and perhaps have a prayer for her. We could not tell what thoughts were hiding behind those dark eyes. One day we got the message that Amelia was much worse and probably would not live through the day. It was quite common for the majority of the community to come to the house of a sick person and just be there. This was their way of showing that they cared.

Amelia's breathing became heavier and unsteady. Finally her eyes closed, her breathing stopped, and everyone thought she was gone. But a few moments later, her eyes opened briefly, and a smile was seen on her countenance. In a very quiet voice, she said, "Jesus, Jesus."

Although Amelia had probably never spoken a word of English, at that moment her eyes were seeing Jesus, and she was liberated from her earthly body. Her soul was received into the arms of Jesus. The Gospel of Jesus Christ works! What a victory! This experience left quite an impression on everyone who was present.

Ivan

I mentioned Ivan Cook earlier. He was the man who drove his boat to our dock and asked me to help him cut logs at the sawmill to build his house.

One day while Ivan and I were working on putting the roof on his home, I asked, "Ivan, do you ever think about God and the things that are taught in the Bible?" This was one of my first attempts to witness to someone individually.

Ivan's abrupt answer was, "I never think about it."

We had the rafters and sheathing on the roof and were ready to put on the roll roofing. We were sitting on the ridge of the roof having a little break when I opened this discussion about spiritual things. With Ivan's abrupt answer, I decided I had said enough for one day.

Time went on and we had a lot of interaction with Ivan and his wife Belle. They had one child, a little girl named Miriam. One day I got a message from Ivan saying, "Can you come over this evening? We need to talk with you." Ivan and Belle were living on an island, so we took the boat and made our way to their house. When we got there, we knocked on the door and then walked in.

They were both crying. We had known that Ivan and his wife had some addiction problems, and it was now clear that they really did need help.

We showed them some Scriptures and explained the plan of salvation. It was a very joyful time as both Ivan and Belle gave their lives to the Lord. It seemed that maybe Ivan had had more thoughts about

God than he admitted when we were on his rooftop. Ivan and Belle continued to grow in their faith, and Ivan eventually even took part in preaching at the church.

Old John

Old John, whose complete name was John Loon, was the oldest person in Slate Falls. He was a very colorful character. Some said he was 106 years old, and a few insisted he was even older. It didn't really matter, as he was certainly over a hundred years old. Most of the time Old John's mind was somewhere else. Only rarely was it in his physical body.

He was always clamoring to go hunting, and his caretakers were kept busy making sure he did not run off. But on those rare occasions when he escaped their watchful eyes, he would come walking up the trail with a big smile on his face. With a stick in his hand, he was ready to go hunting, even if the weather was twenty degrees below zero. Sometimes he would be wearing only a light jacket and have a boot on one foot and a light sneaker on the other.

Everybody in the community knew that when Old John came walking up the trail with that fiendish, childhood grin on his face, he had escaped the watchful eyes of his caretakers. Eventually someone would trick him into going back home, though he had no idea where home was.

Solomon

Solomon was an older man who kept everybody busy trying to figure out where he was going next. He would travel back and forth from Osnaburgh to Slate Falls with bags of things to sell. These bags would contain used clothing, shoes, or cans of Klik, a type of canned meat. He would charter a flight and load everything. When he arrived in Slate Falls, he would pitch his tent and make it known that he has things to sell. Judging by the number of bags he brought, we assumed he was settling in for the whole winter. He always lived in a tent, saying houses were too warm. Even if the weather was thirty below zero, Solomon still liked his tent.

He could speak a little English, and with our bit of Ojibwa, we were able to communicate—at least somewhat. One time he pulled on my beard and asked, "Does white man use medicine to make fur grow?"

Weasel

Another interesting character was an older man always referred to as "Weasel." Nobody seemed to know how he got his nickname. Weasel and his wife were of the old-school natives, traveling all over from Osnaburgh to Slate Falls and on to Cat Lake. Paddling a small canoe, they would make their rounds. Weasel played the violin and enjoyed entertaining everyone with his playing.

One winter when we were in Slate Falls after our main stay, our family was living in a very small cabin and I got sick. It was not a life-threatening sickness, but I had a high fever and it really kept me under the covers. Every day Weasel would stop by, poke his head in the door, and ask Edna, "Did Edwin die yet?"

My wife would reply that I had not died. Weasel's reply was always, "Maybe tomorrow he die."

Chapter 11

The Chase

*L*evius was one of those who was able to manipulate the system. Every so often he would need to get "groceries." Among these, there were usually several large bottles of whiskey, enough to start a full-blown drinking party. One of those parties happened late one October evening. The weather was chilly with a cold mist blowing across Bamadji Lake. Levius had been to town, but nobody seemed to be alarmed, though he was famous for sharing his drinks with the neighbors and having a party.

We had a free evening, so we decided to visit the Jimmy Keesic family. Jimmy was a teacher, and we enjoyed their fellowship a lot. We were having a friendly visit when the door burst open and Levius' wife Charlotte came in. She was bleeding and all out of breath. She had a limited English vocabulary, but we were able to communicate quite well. Barely inside the door, she blurted out, "They are really fighting. Much drinking. Come quickly!" There were no police available, so whenever there was trouble they came to get the preacher, which was me.

Charlotte informed us that Levius, John Lee, Rex, and Lewis were drunk and were fighting. We knew this was a bad combination! Of the men she mentioned, Lewis was the main one we were concerned about, as he had a reputation as a hothead. John Lee was a harmless elderly man with dementia, while Rex was a young man whom we didn't really consider dangerous. Charlotte explained that the ruckus was in a tent way back in the forest.

A young couple living close to the Keesics named George and Ruby had requested that we come to their house later in the evening to discuss spiritual matters. We were looking forward to doing so, but now it seemed we would be breaking up a drinking party instead. (Satan sure has a clever way of distracting us from good things.) Jimmy and I talked it over briefly and decided we needed additional help, so we decided to go ask George if he would go along.

Walking through the forest on a narrow footpath in the pitch darkness was not exactly how we wanted to spend the evening, but the three of us started off, not knowing what to expect. We went to Levius' house first, but everything was quiet there. We decided maybe it was happening at John Lee's tent. John Lee was a kind old man when he was sober, and being a typical old-timer, he was more at home in a tent than a house. We tried to be as quiet as possible and finally found the footpath that led to his tent. We were expecting a lot of noise and fighting, but when we arrived everything was completely quiet. However, we sensed that someone was there.

Talking in whispers, George and Jimmy nominated me to open the tent flap to see if anyone was there. I was scared. We had heard stories of how violent these men could be when intoxicated. I checked to see if my flashlight was working, then gingerly opened the tent flap to peek in. What I saw seemed incredible. The small barrel stove was thrown over, with the stovepipe lying nearby, and smoke was pouring into the tent. As my eyes adjusted to the smoke, I saw a man lying on his back on a cot. The fire was still flickering, and I could see blood flowing across the dirt floor of the tent.

As my eyes adjusted, I saw two men lying on the ground almost at my feet, the one on top of the other in a bear hug. I managed to find my voice, "Okay, friends. What is going on?"

Quick as a flash, the voice of Lewis spoke out, "Yeah, preacher, we hear you." We did not like having Lewis in the mix, he being one who always turned violent when intoxicated. He was the one who would be searching for guns. He was the one who would be "out to kill" when intoxicated.

I quickly considered my options, and they weren't too great. When I turned around to discuss our strategy with George and Jimmy, they were gone, having heard Lewis talking. By that time, Lewis was on his feet, quite lively, and he let me know that he was coming to get me. He picked up a stick the size of a two-by-four and came running for me. I could run as fast as anybody my age, and I certainly had no desire to get caught in a fight, so I quickly decided running would be the best choice.

I had some advantages over my pursuer. For one, I was not

intoxicated, giving me a bit more "brain power." And I had a flashlight that I could switch on in case I needed it, although it would be a giveaway to keep it on. I also had several friends to help me—only right now they were not around!

I knew this portion of trails very well, so I tried to put as much distance between Lewis and myself as possible. I soon discovered another advantage I had—I didn't holler and scream expletives, letting the world know where I was going. I would turn my flashlight on quickly to get my bearings, then I would turn it off again and keep going. Meanwhile, Lewis would come to a log he did not see and trip over it. I could easily tell where he was going by the cursing echoing through the night.

I was getting winded from running, but I realized that I had better keep going because I didn't exactly want to have that two-by-four imbedded in my head. I made kind of a half circle with a goal in mind: I would aim for my old woodshed—a ten- by twelve-foot log shack where I stored my dry firewood. It had a hook on the inside, so I could lock the door. I complimented myself for thinking of that.

I went inside and found a crack in the logs where I could peek out and keep track of where my pursuer was going. I was just getting positioned when I heard someone breathing in the other corner of the woodshed. I soon discovered that the other tenant was George. We both chuckled quietly and tried our best to get a lead on where Lewis might be.

George and I listened carefully and could hear Lewis coming our way. We watched as he ran past the woodshed and straight to the back door of our house. *My, I'm glad I locked that door,* I thought. There was a small enclosed porch that led into the main part of the house. I knew he could likely open the porch door but not the one leading into the house. But it was taking too long, and I didn't hear a thing. "I better go see what's going on," I told George. Cautiously I opened the woodshed door to exit the shed. My, those hinges squeaked! I slowly made my way across the open area to our house. To my alarm, I found both doors open. My pursuer was inside our house!

I tiptoed through the house on the first story, but no Lewis. Finally I had enough courage to check the upstairs. I could not believe what I found. Lewis was in our bedroom, face down in a puddle of vomit, fast asleep! I suppose he was as tired from chasing me as I was running away from him.

I knew this would not be a good time to wake him up, so I tiptoed down and outside again.

When I got outside, I found quite a few of our neighbors who had heard about the chase and were there to help. I made it clear that I did not want Lewis waking up in our bedroom because I had some guns in the closet.

It was now around midnight and pitch dark. It was also dark spiritually, with a strange, eerie atmosphere reminding us that Satan is real and was having a ball tonight. By this time, the village was beginning to wake up with all the commotion going on. We finally found a few volunteers brave enough to go into the house to bring Lewis outside until he sobered up. This proved to be more difficult than anybody had thought. He was finally subdued and tied to a tree.

While all this was transpiring, other activities were going on at the tent where the chase began. The other two partiers woke up when Lewis took off, and it was soon obvious that Levius was hurt badly.

While we were dealing with Lewis, Rex took Levius to his home. He attempted to break down Levius' door with his fist. The problem was, the door was stronger than his fist, and he ended up breaking several bones in his hand.

During all of this, my family had been patiently waiting at the Keesic home. When Jimmy had arrived back home, he had told them some of what was going on, but they didn't know the whole story until I arrived. We soon found out that the commotion wasn't over yet when there was a sharp knock at the door. As we looked up in alarm, Lewis stepped inside. Our children went dashing like mice at a cat convention, looking for a hiding place. I was speechless. I looked at the beat-up hulk in the doorway and wondered if he would finish the job he had set out to accomplish—kill the preacher! I had no place to run and he was blocking the only exit.

But Lewis's mood had changed. Now the alcohol had turned him silly. We listened to some of his ridiculous tales as we wondered how to get this fellow out of the house. Jimmy finally managed to get him outside and took him to the telephone booth to call his girlfriend. While going down the muddy footpath, they met a neighbor man Lewis didn't like. Soon they were fighting it out, rolling around in the mud—and using language as thick and foul as mud. Finally Lewis was cornered and tied up.

But now we had another complication. A messenger came and told Edna that Levius was back at his home and was badly hurt. Because Edna was the community healthcare representative, she had the responsibility of managing this, but we knew if we sent Levius to the hospital, he would bring back more "firewater." Besides, it was now around 2:00 in the morning, and the only way to get him to a hospital was by bush plane. Edna decided to wait until morning. He would have to endure his beat-up body until dawn.

When we arrived at the cabin where Levius lived, we found the majority of the community somehow crammed into his little one-room log cabin. The cabin was approximately sixteen by twenty feet. Carrying flashlights, lanterns, and a few kerosene lamps, we were finally able to shove our way through the crowded room to the bedside where a body lay that was so beat up and mutilated that we would have been clueless who it was. The strangeness of the whole scenario made me pinch myself, questioning whether I was really here or dreaming. The eerie feeling in this little crowded room with people, tobacco smoke, large bottles of alcohol, sweat, and blood finally brought us to reality.

When we looked at Levius lying on a narrow cot in the corner of the room, breathing heavily and moaning and groaning with every breath he took, we noticed that his face looked very much like hamburger. His one eye looked like it was partially detached. Everything was bloody. Satanic powers were obvious everywhere.

As the first rays of dawn were beginning to light the eastern sky, Edna and I left Levius' house and headed for home. We were tired beyond measure, but deep inside we felt satisfied because we had done what we could and had done it for the Lord.

Later that morning Edna and I wearily made the half-mile trek to the house where the community phone was. It was sometimes very difficult to get our calls through on the community phone. You had to lift the receiver and wait (patiently) until an operator somewhere three hundred miles away decided to answer the little light that lit up on the switchboard. And before any communication took place, the operator's voice had to go from Thunder Bay to somewhere halfway to the moon, bounce off a satellite, and land in my telephone. It's amazing that it even worked. Once a connection was made, we would tell the operator what phone number we wished to call. Sometimes it went through quickly; other times we would hear, "Come back in an hour and try again!" During the warm summer weather, it was not too bad to wait, but in the winter months the temperature might be thirty below, and waiting was not very appealing.

This morning it was good. The phone was available immediately, the operator had a good dose of strong coffee, and the voices were clear. Edna was soon speaking to a doctor about the beaten-up man we had on our hands. She explained that under the circumstances it might be better to send a doctor to Slate Falls and do the repair work here instead of flying the injured man to the hospital and taking a chance of him getting more alcohol, bringing it home, and starting another party. This could just keep on going!

The doctor replied, "We will see what we can work out. Call back in a half hour." While waiting the half hour, people who happened to be near the phone kept asking questions. "What happened last night? How is Levius? When will you take him out? Do you have an escort to go with him?" We answered the questions the best we could until we finally got an answer from the hospital. "A plane will be there in an hour and a half with a doctor," they told us. This was great news!

The floatplane landed at our dock, and we led the doctor to the cabin where Levius was lying on a cot. He seemed only half conscious, but he did respond to the questions the doctor asked. The doctor did a bit of checking but told us that he needs to go to the hospital. His injuries were too serious to repair him here. It took several days for the community to get back to normal. Levius eventually recovered and came home to Slate Falls.

Levius Has a Visitor

Even after Levius returned home, this whole incident weighed heavily on our minds. We requested prayer from friends who had an interest in our work and purposed as a family to have a day of prayer and fasting for Levius. The morning after our day of prayer, still quite early, there was a knock on our door. I was surprised to see Levius there. He was sober and subdued. We chatted about various things, but it was obvious that he had something more on his mind. After an extended pause, he cleared his throat. Without looking at anybody, he said, "I had a dream last night." It was very common to have people share their dreams with us. There were times when I felt like Daniel must have felt when the king demanded he interpret a dream he could no longer remember. I had an advantage, however: Levius remembered very well what he had dreamed!

He told us about his dream, saying, "I woke up in the middle of the night, and there was light in the cabin. Standing by my bedside was a man dressed in white. He looked at me with the kindest eyes and said something like this: 'If you don't eat the flesh of the Son of Man and drink His blood, you have no life in you. If you do this, I will raise you up at the last day.' " Then Levius asked, "What does this mean?"

Even though Levius had this quotation from the Bible somewhat mixed up, it was definitely from John 6:53-56. Wow!

Why am I surprised? I wondered. We had been praying that God would open Levius' eyes. In fact, we had just had a day of prayer and fasting. This was God's way of answering our prayers and giving Levius another chance to repent.

I took my time to answer his question. I showed him the Scripture in the Bible where this was found. Then I took a deep breath. "Levius, I believe Jesus was at your bedside. He is calling you to change your life and follow Him. God is trying to get your attention. You were really beaten up in that last party you had. This could be your final call. You might not live through another such calamity. You might be killed."

Levius stared at the carpet under his feet, not saying a word nor showing any emotion. I could almost feel the weight of indecision in his mind. Finally he got to his feet, shook my hand, and went out the door. I went to the back room and watched him slowly walking the little footpath that led through the forest to his house. It was such a lonely picture—an old man with a heavy load on his back.

Four weeks later we got a message: Levius Wesley had been found in a back alley in Sioux Lookout. He had been beaten to death. He had waited too long. He had rejected a special call from God. We will never know what his last thoughts were. Perhaps he died slowly and had time to repent. He knew what it takes to accept Jesus. It was a sad day in Slate Falls.

Chapter 12

Wilderness Surprise

*I*t was one of those winter days when you are not sure if you should get out of bed or just stay put. I was in Red Lake for some meetings. After the meetings were over, I was scheduled to fly back to Slate Falls. I had been away for several days and did not like to be away from my wife and children too long. I longed to be on my way because I knew how quickly and unexpectedly things can change with flights.

The weather had been quite unpredictable, and I hardly dared look out the window, fearing the weather might not be conducive for flying. Special services were scheduled for Slate Falls the next day and Ivan Ramer was the pastor who would conduct the services. Ivan lived in Red Lake, so it was only logical that I would fly with him from Red Lake to Slate Falls.

Eager as I was to get home, I knew there was no point in pushing the issue. If the weather wasn't flyable, you just "ain't goin' nowhere." A motto in the office said it plainly: "There are old pilots, and there are bold pilots, but there are no old, bold pilots." I finally built up enough courage to look out the window, and I did not like what I saw. Fog and light snow flurries just weren't what we had wished for. I had explained in detail to God what kind of weather we needed. Maybe He hadn't understood me correctly.

Now and then during the forenoon, the cloud cover would lift slightly, but then it always returned. Finally, around 2:00 in the afternoon, Ivan decided the weather was good enough to fly. If it turned nasty again, we could always turn around and come back to Red Lake. It was around 2:30 when our little Piper Cub J-3 bounced across the drifted snow in Howie Bay and picked up speed until we were airborne. There was more wind than I had hoped for, and the little craft had about all it could manage.

Flying in the bush is limited to visual flying. We did not need much altitude to clear the treetops, but it is dangerous to fly at only five hundred feet because there is not much room to drop if needed. The steady hum of the little canvas-covered craft sounded reassuring enough. Even the occasional gusts of wind that seemed to overpower us were predictable enough to provide a sense of security. We were flying at an altitude of eight hundred feet over Confederation Lake when Ivan pointed to the windshield. Ice was forming. This was not good. Nothing can make an aircraft gain weight like ice. It can also change the airflow over the wings.

Turning back to Red Lake was not an option, as we were over halfway to Slate Falls already. We tried to fly higher to get out of the fog, but it was all to no avail. Finally Ivan looked at me over the top of his glasses and asked, "Do you see any nice cozy spot to lay our pillow for the night?" It was already dusk in the deep north. Landing on skis in three feet of unpacked snow had its own set of troubles that neither of us liked. But by now, there was no other option, so we headed downward.

We tried to find a spot where the snow looked soft and cozy. The landing was smooth, and we taxied to a small island some distance ahead, stopped the engine, and enjoyed the comfort and warmth of the small aircraft for a few more minutes. Ivan explained the procedure of putting the plane to bed. In the back of the plane were some light canvas covers for the wings. After this was done, we took an old comforter and stuffed it all around the engine, pushing it into every nook and cranny. Underneath the engine was a little door in the cowling where we put a small infrared heater. After we were sure the heater was burning nicely and safely, we looked around. Where should we settle down?

It was now nearly dark, and as far as we could see there was no civilization within forty miles. But suddenly we heard something that sounded like a human voice. Then we heard it again, and we were certain it was a human voice. We looked in the direction we thought it was coming from, and sure enough, about a hundred yards away was an old man struggling through the deep snow toward us. We wondered what kind of human being could be stomping around out here in the deep snow.

The man extended his hand in welcome. He was a short, stocky

Wilderness Surprise

man and spoke with a heavy accent, which we soon discovered was German. Even though Ivan and I both spoke Pennsylvania Dutch, we found it more comfortable to speak English. He briefly introduced himself as Karl Kochier and said he lived in a shack close by. He assured us that we were welcome to stay with him for the night, and his wife would be happy to cook a meal for us. A wife? Did we hear right? This old prospector had a wife living in this wilderness?

We followed him up a steep bank and there on a little knoll was a house. It was actually an old house trailer. Karl and his wife Polly did everything in their means to make us feel comfortable and welcome. Their life was certainly an interesting one. Karl was a German who had been in Hitler's army in World War II. When he saw things going the wrong direction in the war, he somehow escaped from the military and found his way to Canada. He decided to be a prospector for gold and lived in the wilderness. "I decided there must be some place on God's earth where a man could live in peace!" By now, he had lived in the wilderness for twenty-four years. He had lived there alone for seventeen years, but then once when he was in Sioux Lookout to get some supplies, he met Polly. She was a teacher at the University of Montreal.

Apparently Polly had become somewhat disenchanted with her life, and so in one week's time Karl and Polly decided to get married. She thought his life in the bush sounded quite glamorous. Karl explained it like this: "You are looking at two failures. I had it in my mind that I would teach Polly to live the way I lived, and Polly planned to house train me. We both planned to live happily ever after. We both failed, but now we have a sort of compromise and are happy together."

They had been married seven years and seemed to enjoy each other. They were living in the area to look after some things for the gold mining company. There had been an active mine here at one point, but it had been shut down. There was still some equipment that the mining company wished to protect, so they offered Karl and Polly some compensation if they would look after the mine's equipment.

We were there for only a short time when we smelled a delicious scent coming from the kitchen. Polly was cooking a full-course dinner for us. It truly was a top-class meal. While Polly cooked, Karl told stories, and we listened and enjoyed them all. It was obvious that Karl and Polly were eager to meet anyone who happened to cross their path.

Karl had stories that lasted most of the night. One of these happened before he got married. Karl had cabins in different areas, so when hunting was not so good anymore in one area, he would pack up and go to another camp in a different location.

One hot summer day he decided to move to a different cabin. He had almost everything he owned on his back. When a sudden thunderstorm came up, he was drenched from head to toe. Knowing there was no one around, he undressed, started a fire, and arranged some branches to hang up his clothes to dry. While waiting for them to dry, Karl fell asleep. Sometime later he awoke with a start. "Something is not right," his senses told him. While Karl slept, the fire had picked up, and all his clothes had been burned. His shoes were still standing there, but when he went to pick them up, they just crumbled.

What do you do when you are stark naked out in the wilderness with millions of mosquitoes? He had no food, no clothes, no way to communicate—and not even shoes to go anywhere. As he fabricated a little shelter of branches, he racked his brain wondering how he would get out of this fix. He could not think of anyone who traveled this area. Days went by and nothing changed. He managed to snag a few fish, but otherwise things looked pretty bleak. Finally one day he heard a boat motor somewhere on the other side of the lake. Sure enough, soon a boat came into view with two fishermen who were exploring new territory.

Karl tried to make himself as presentable as possible (which wasn't very presentable) and went to the shoreline, waving his arms and running back and forth. The motor slowed down, and he could sense exactly what was going through the men's minds: "What is that crazy man doing out here in the Canadian wilderness, running around naked?" After some contemplation, the boat turned around and went in the direction it had come from. Karl assumed they were gone for good. He nearly cursed them, but then realized they could not be blamed.

Then, about two days later, Karl heard the drone of another motor. This time it was a floatplane, the Ontario Provincial Police. They circled, then landed on the lake and taxied to Karl—the "wild bush man," as the fishermen had described him. They docked their plane and just sat and laughed for a while. It was easy for the police to see that Karl was telling the truth. Actually, Karl knew the one policeman. They gave him a free ride to Red Lake and bought some clothes while Karl waited in the aircraft.

Karl's stories were very interesting, but Ivan and I finally suggested we should probably get some shut-eye before morning. We slept warmly that night. The next morning, after eating a hearty breakfast in Polly's kitchen, we thanked them for their hospitality and offered to pay them. But they refused to take anything, saying we must obey the rules of the north: "Someday you will come across someone else who needs help, then you help them!" We were impressed with their hospitality. They certainly made it possible for us to rest in comfort. We had been prepared to sleep in the plane, or maybe even in the snow.

Chapter 13

Stranded!

"Edna, you must get up and move around."

Her answer was a weak, mumbling, "Just let me rest a bit longer." Edna and I were in a life-threatening situation.

It was late February. Edna and I had decided to take our Escapade snowmobile and visit our friends in Cat Lake for several days. The weather was very cold, but that is when the trails are at their best. We left Slate Falls on a Monday morning and arrived at Cat Lake shortly before noon. We got a warm reception from the people. We planned to stay there several days, then travel back to Slate Falls on Wednesday.

We were a bit concerned about slush. The lakes might have two feet of ice, but whenever there is a heavy snowfall, the weight of the newly fallen snow pushes down the ice. When this happens, water rises to the top of the ice. From the bottom of the lake you have water, then ice, then a thin layer of water, and then snow on top of all that. This formula equals slush—and slush and snowmobiles are not very compatible.

Sure enough, the day before we left Cat Lake, it snowed nearly all day, giving us plenty of reason to be concerned about slush on the larger lakes. The problem is, you cannot see areas of slush until you drive into them. You will rarely encounter slush if you stay on a well-packed trail, but a heavy snow with wind will rearrange the snow, and you cannot see the trail anymore.

On Wednesday morning as we packed our things onto a small sled pulled by our snowmobile, we were pleased that it was not snowing anymore, but we were well aware of the potential of encountering slush. We left Cat Lake at 11:00. The temperature was thirty below zero with a slight breeze, promising to increase. We had made many trips back and forth from Slate Falls to Cat Lake, but it was still an adventure to travel those sixty-five miles through endless forests and lakes without any means of communication. Stories are told of people freezing to death or getting attacked by packs of hungry timber wolves.

It was around 1:00 when we reached Zion's Lake. Some people claim Zion's Lake is bewitched, and it did seem that whenever there was trouble it happened on that lake. We had developed the habit of stopping the engine and having prayer before we started to cross the ten-mile expanse.

By that time the wind had picked up, and it had started to snow again. We were about twenty minutes onto the lake when it became obvious that we were no longer on the packed trail. Then, all of a sudden, it happened. The snowmobile hit a patch of slush and quickly bogged down as it sank into the snow and water. We also sank into a feeling of hopelessness and helplessness.

I stepped out of the machine and sank down into the water. The water was deeper than my boots, so they quickly filled with ice-cold water. Edna was still sitting on the machine, vowing that she was not stepping into that water. Our choices were quite limited because we were thirty miles from any place of refuge and hopelessly stuck in the slush. Not only that, but the winds were reaching thirty miles per hour, the shoreline was a mile away, and the daylight hours were limited. The realization was starting to sink in that nobody knew where we were. The people in Cat Lake knew we had left at about lunchtime, but they had no reason to know we were in trouble. Only God knew.

I finally persuaded Edna to leave the comparative safety of the snowmobile, and she reluctantly stepped into the slushy mess. We began our walk across the lake in snow that reached our waist and slush that reached the tops of our boots. After only a short walk, we realized that this could be serious. We stomped along one miserable step at a time.

We plodded along for about an hour, and the shoreline was still far away. Then we both heard it. In the distance, a snowmobile was coming from the direction of Cat Lake, driving on the same trail we had been on. As we watched and waved, the man drove into the same slush we had gotten stuck in. He was a quarter of a mile away, and as he struggled to get out of the slush, he finally succeeded. He had a much lighter machine than we did and was able to lift his machine and turn it around. Thankfully, he had seen us, and with no great trouble he soon reached us.

His small machine was barely able to carry even one passenger, so there was no chance of us riding with him. He told us he was going to Slate Falls, and he promised to go there as fast as he could, which wasn't very fast. He said he would send someone to rescue us. As he drove off, we wondered if he would get stuck somewhere else, or if he would remember to send someone. By this time, daylight was fast departing and we still had quite a distance to the shore. I assumed once we got there, we could maybe start a fire, or at least be off the wind.

It was almost dark when we reached the tree-covered island. We could hardly walk anymore. Our boots were encased with ice, which made our feet about twice as heavy as usual. It felt good to be on dry land, but it didn't change the fact that the temperature was still about thirty below, the wind still blew, and it was now completely dark. It also didn't change the fact that our life depended on how successful the lone traveler was in reaching Slate Falls and in sending someone to rescue us. But with God all things are possible.

We did have a small axe and a blanket. The axe was useful in knocking the ice off our boots, and the blanket could be wrapped around our shoulders for some protection from the cold. But it was soon evident that starting a fire was impossible. How could we find any dry kindling that could be lit in this wind and snow?

Knowing we had to keep moving, Edna and I made a path approximately one hundred feet into the forest. We stomped our feet and walked back and forth to stay as warm as possible. We were getting so tired we could hardly move anymore. Every so often we would spread our blanket on the snow and lie down to relax our muscles for a few minutes. But we soon discovered the danger of this. It felt so good that we could hardly persuade each other to get up again. I have heard that freezing to death is one of the most painless ways to die.

As the darkness had now fully engulfed us, we did some calculating on the soonest we could expect help from Slate Falls. In the meantime, we tried to keep our thoughts on positive things. We looked up and marveled at the beauty of a starlit sky. On any night close to residential areas, it is surprising how much light is reflected into the sky. But we were hundreds of miles from any city, and it was dark—really dark!

And so we walked and stomped, and stomped and walked. Sometimes we laughed, and sometimes we cried. Sometimes we yelled at each other to get up and keep walking. As we walked back and forth, we kept watching for lights coming from the south. Sometimes we were sure we heard something, but it was just another illusion. It was now past the time we thought rescuers could arrive.

Slowly the evening wore on. We were not terribly cold because we were wearing good warm clothes. But fatigue was making us feel like giving up. Most of the time we were serious, but then we would get almost silly, thinking about food. We had not eaten all day.

It is interesting how a mind will function at a time like this. Many times we would pause because we were sure we heard an engine or saw a flicker of light in the distance, only to realize that our mind and imagination had fooled us again. We also imagined we heard wolves.

Finally, at around 9:00, we really did see a light coming in the distance—two lights, actually! How we rejoiced! The police from Slate

Falls came with two snowmobiles. They offered us the one, and they would ride double on the other. We still had over an hour of driving on the snowmobile, which is a very cold ride. But at least we were headed in the right direction!

The house we lived in was heated by a wood stove, so it was totally cold when we arrived home around midnight. I tried to start a fire as quickly as possible, but it took some time until the stove was radiating much heat.

We had been out in the cold twelve hours with water in our boots. In fact, we couldn't remove our boots until the ice melted. It proved to be a blessing that the house was cold. We did have some frostbite but nothing serious. As cold as we were, going into a warm house could have caused severe frostbite. We went to bed thanking the Lord for being alive. And believe it or not, we went to bed on our empty stomachs.

After falling into bed and sleeping for about two hours, we both had nightmares. We woke up absolutely terrified, thinking we were still out on the lake. This happened every night for almost a week.

The following day we made plans to get our snowmobile. I asked several friends to go bring it home. It was not terribly difficult. When slush is exposed to the cold, it will freeze. The men took a spud bar along and chopped the snowmobile loose, then they were able to lay it on its side, chop the ice out of the track area, and drive home.

Getting stuck on Zion's Lake was an experience we will never forget.

Chapter 14

A Powerful God

Mildred was the youngest daughter of Monroe and Maxine. She was used to having things her way, and it showed. Mildred's mother was a Christian and had deep concerns about her daughter. One Sunday evening Maxine begged her daughter to go along to church, but Mildred wasn't interested. She made a few negative comments and made it clear that she had more important things to do, such as cleaning the house and listening to music. But as Maxine left the house, Mildred shoved some money into her mother's hand and said, "Give this to the mission. I will buy my way to heaven. I don't understand the Bible anyway. It doesn't make sense."

With a heavy heart, Mildred's mother slowly walked the quarter mile to the little church, wondering what it would take to break her daughter's rebellious spirit. Meanwhile, back at home, unusual things began happening. Mildred was cleaning the house and playing her music when suddenly the music stopped. In the back room of the little cabin, Mildred heard something drop. *That's strange,* she thought. *It isn't windy, and there is no one else in the house. I'd better go check it out.*

Mildred's mother was one of the few ladies in the village who still did beadwork, such as moccasins and mitts with fancy decorations. The best way to handle these tiny beads was to put them in a little pan. Mildred had just finished cleaning the back room, so she clearly remembered her mother's well-worn Bible on a stand by the window. And on top of the Bible was the pan of tiny beads. As Mildred entered the room, she felt something strange, like a sacred presence. She stood there, more or less awestruck, as she observed the rearrangement of certain items. The pan of beads was still on the table, with none of them spilled, but the Bible was lying on the floor, open. She distinctly remembered that the beads had been on top of the Bible. *How could the Bible have slid out from under the pan of beads without spilling them?* she wondered.

She picked up the Bible and this is what her eyes fell on: "Why do ye not understand my speech? even because ye cannot hear my word? Ye are of your father the devil, and the lusts of your father ye will do. He was a murderer from the beginning, and abode not in the truth, because there is no truth in him" (John 8:43, 44). Mildred was spellbound. Had God sent an angel to open the Bible so she would understand? Mildred knew that God was speaking to her. She sent a message to her mother at church: "Come home quickly. I need to talk to someone."

The implications were obvious. Mildred remembered telling her mother that she didn't understand the Bible. Now Jesus was telling her in His own words why she didn't understand. It was a real battle for Mildred to be willing to make this commitment, but finally, with many people praying, she came through.

There were still struggles, however. Monroe, Mildred's father, was not a Christian at the time. One day as he listened to a conversation between Mildred and her mother and other believers, he thought they called him a devil and got very upset.

We spent hours explaining to Monroe that we were talking about a quote from the Bible and were not talking about him. Communicating with Monroe was a challenge. He spoke English fairly well, but I am not sure if the Ojibwa language has a word that specifically means "forgiveness." As I knelt in front of Monroe begging for forgiveness, I described it the best I could. He finally responded, "Let's just forget about it."

The Bible makes it clear that we must forgive one another. We take that as actually asking each other for forgiveness. Among the natives here, we noticed a different way that seems to work. When they wish to forgive, they bring a gift of some kind. Giving the offended person a large piece of moose meat is very effective in applying for forgiveness!

Monroe later accepted the Lord. He is now ninety-six years old, and we are best friends. It is sad to say, but Mildred is still struggling spiritually. Her desire is to be a victorious Christian, but that's not always the case. Many people are praying for her, and I believe her day will come.

God Answers a Prayer

Nancy was Canasia's niece. One day she came to our house with a request. Nancy's request was quite simple. "Auntie Canasia borrowed $45 from me six months ago. I suppose she forgot all about it, but I really need the money. Would you please talk to her and remind her that I need the money next week?"

This was not exactly in my comfort zone, but I told her we would think about it.

As I thought about it, I decided to "pass the buck." Maybe Jesus would like to do something for Nancy, as so far she had not shown much interest in spiritual things. So our family prayed about it, asking the Lord to remind Canasia to give back the money she owed to Nancy.

We almost forgot the whole incident until about a week later when I met Nancy on the boardwalk. "Hey, thanks for talking to Canasia about the money," she said. "She volunteered to pay it back the day after I talked to you."

It is interesting that during the six months after the money was borrowed, the two ladies had never discussed the money. But Jesus reminded Canasia about the money the day after we prayed for her to be reminded. I never told Nancy that I did not speak to Canasia about their money problems. I didn't think it was necessary. God had answered our prayer.

Demons

In the New Testament, Jesus encountered many demons, or devils, and He was very capable of casting them out. The idea that there are demons in our time seems rather absurd to many people, even to the point of causing rifts in friendships and churches. In Slate Falls, it was not unusual to have people speak of demons. When we came across this, it was usually in an area where Satan had strongholds for many years.

People sometimes asked us to come and pray over their house, saying they heard voices in the house. Or sometimes their doors would open and close with nobody visibly doing it. There were many incidents like this that proved Satan is still at work.

When the all-weather road was built from Sioux Lookout to Slate Falls, approximately one hundred miles through forests and around lakes, the men from our reserve built most of it. They did a wonderful job, working long, hard hours, even at night. As strange as it may sound, the biggest obstacle they encountered was demons. The men were regularly seeing images they considered demons, and it wasn't just one person seeing them. It became serious enough that some of the men refused to work on the night shift. The chief at that time was not a Christian, but he asked the mission people to pray and cast out the demons that were harassing the workers.

This was quite a challenge! It wasn't that we didn't believe God was still on the throne and could meet such challenges. We just knew that Satan had a stronghold in this area. Still, we put up a notice that at a certain time we would have a special prayer time out in the bush where these sightings were most prevalent. We had no idea who would show up, or if anyone would show up. We cultivated our faith as much as we knew how, and at the appointed time people started to show up. We had twenty people there of all descriptions—some skeptics, some believers.

We tried to explain to the people that the reason they saw demons was because they invited them. Many of them lived in sin and immorality, using drugs, alcohol, and such. Because they tolerated such practices, the devil felt quite welcome. We explained that we weren't doing anything magical by praying. We were simply acknowledging what was happening, and we were petitioning God to show His power to rid this area from the demons. We explained that we would join hands and form a big prayer circle. We invited them to be part of the prayer circle even if they weren't Christians—but they had to believe that God was powerful enough to cast out the demons. All but three people joined hands. We explained again that they were recognizing that God was superior and all-powerful.

In the days of Nebuchadnezzar, the Hebrew captives answered like this: "If it be so, our God whom we serve is able to deliver us from the burning fiery furnace, and He will deliver us out of thine hand, 0 king. But if not, be it known unto thee, 0 king, that we will not serve thy gods, nor worship the golden image which thou hast set up" (Daniel 3:17, 18).

Those who were Christians prayed along with us. It was a very touching experience. Not one person made fun of this prayer meeting. And it put an end to the spirits harassing the workers. Once again God confirmed that He truly is all-powerful and almighty. God be praised!

Chapter 15

Alex

Alex was a colorful character in the community. His sense of humor was something to get used to. If anyone new arrived in the community, you could be sure Alex had a different name for the person every day. He might be Levi today and Andy tomorrow. He would pretend he had never met the person before.

Alex was exceptionally smart. He spoke perfect English and even picked up a few German words. He ran a trapline in the winter and was happy to take visitors along if they wanted to.

Alex's expertise at fishing was almost unbelievable. He could catch fish even if no one else could. Jacob Miller was a driver who frequently brought visitors to Slate Falls, and he loved to fish. Jacob took some pride in his own fishing abilities, yet he told me about a time he witnessed Alex fishing. "I was fishing for the greater part of a day with no fish to speak of when Alex came out of nowhere with his boat and anchored close by. I watched as he prepared his line, and in less than five minutes he was pulling in a beautiful pickerel. He kept on catching fish until he had about a dozen nice walleyes flopping around in his boat. Then he pulled up his anchor and roared off!"

Alex had ten children and a hardworking wife, Molly. He also had a problem: he was an alcoholic. He tried hard to overcome his habit and sometimes succeeded for several months, but then it would start again. As can be expected, when he was under the influence, his character changed from fun-loving, cheerful, and humorous to angry and disagreeable. When he was in this situation, everybody stayed away until he sobered up again.

Alex helped at the school as a teacher's aide. The school at Slate Falls was a government-funded school where our children also attended. One morning Alex came to school drunk. On this particular day, I was to attend meetings in Red Lake. Before I left on the plane for the hour-long flight to Red Lake, I told my wife that our children should not go to school until Alex has overcome his addiction. I flew off without giving any thought to the repercussions this decision would generate.

As soon as word spread through the community that we were taking our children out of school, it became the gossip of the week. My timing was very bad, making such a statement and leaving my family alone to face the issue. People were so upset that we decided to move my wife and children to Stormer Lake until things quieted down. It was a traumatic experience for our family.

Stormer Lake is a counseling center where people can come and stay for a week or so. It was usually full in the winter months, but thankfully a cabin was available when we needed it. On the day my family was brought to that little cabin at Stormer Lake, I was there to meet them. I cannot recall ever feeling so discouraged as when my wife and children related all the details of their unplanned getaway. We just knelt around a little table and cried.

We had goals of being at Slate Falls for the long term, yet here we were in a little log cabin in the northern wilderness with no native people around. Was our call and commitment only imagination? Should we load up our possessions and head back to Ohio? Our earnest prayers seemed to have no answers.

After our first wave of prayers and tears, I begged the Lord for forgiveness for the poor timing without considering people's reaction. I opened the Bible at random without any Scripture in mind. The very first verses we laid eyes on was 1 Peter 4:12-14:

> Beloved, think it not strange concerning the fiery trial which is to try you, as though some strange thing happened unto you: But rejoice, inasmuch as ye are partakers of Christ's sufferings; that, when His glory shall be revealed, ye may be glad also with exceeding joy. If ye be reproached for the name of Christ, happy are ye; for the spirit of glory, and of God resteth upon you: on their part he is evil spoken of, but on your part, he is glorified.

We all rejoiced. What more could we expect! This was like a special answer from God. We all felt like new people. It was a reassurance that God was listening, watching every detail of our life. God is so good!

During our time at Stormer Lake, we helped with the work there while still keeping some contact with the people at Slate Falls. Little by little we began to sense a softening among the offended people, and one day we got an official invitation from them, saying, "We want you to come back." Within several days, we were flying back to Slate Falls. We were still nervous and wondered how our reception would be. When we got back, we had several community meetings and the offended people agreed to "give it a try."

There were moments of tension but nothing serious. As we walked the narrow trails from day to day, we still hoped we would not meet certain people who had been the most upset. Occasionally we would meet someone who looked the other way when we passed each other. But time has a way of healing, or at least taking the edge off difficult situations. It took several months, however, before we felt comfortable in Alex's presence.

One Saturday afternoon Alex came home from town and we were informed that he was under the influence again and had slipped and fallen on the ice and hurt his back. I decided this would be a good time to visit him. I went to his bedside and talked to him. It was pretty much a one-sided conversation, but it was a start. A week went by and it was obvious Alex would not be teaching school anytime soon. Sometimes when a teacher had several days off, they would ask our daughter Virginia to fill in as substitute teacher, which she was happy to do. Knowing that it would be several weeks until Alex's back would heal sufficiently, we offered our services to have Virginia substitute until Alex was able to return to the classroom.

During this time we had been praying that something would develop so we could have normal communications with Alex and his family. God showed us what we should do. Since the school was an official government school, they paid the teachers well. Naturally, the paychecks were sent to us for Virginia, and they were sizeable amounts. We decided we should give the money to Alex.

I remember struggling with the idea at first because we were "poor missionaries" and could use some extra cash. I well remember the day I carried the first paycheck to Alex's house. I knew this was the right thing to do, but I still did not "feel" the love I should have—until I put the check into Alex's shaking hand.

At first he flatly refused to accept it, but I insisted. Alex repeatedly said, "Edwin, I can't do this." When I left Alex's house that day, I was the happiest man around. Now I "felt" love. It was a real lesson for me. If you know the right thing to do, do it, even if you don't feel like it. The feelings will come later.

This was the beginning of a change in our relationship with Alex's family. Once again it was comfortable to visit in their home, and they did not hesitate to come and visit us. A few months later, one of Alex's children came to our house carrying a crumpled, dirty piece of paper with a note written on it. It said, "Dad wants you to come to our house." At first I was scared. *What does he want?* I wondered. *Does he want to retaliate?* I had heard rumors that Alex was drinking again. After discussing it with my family, I left the house and walked the quarter mile to Alex's house.

I knocked on the door and heard a weak voice telling me to come in. It was rather dark in the house, but I finally found my way to a back room. There, lying on a cot, somewhat propped up with blankets and pillows, was Alex. He was sober, but I could tell that he had been drinking earlier.

He was also crying. As I took his hand, my tears also started to flow. Alex finally gained his composure enough to say, "I can't go on living like this. Do you think God and my friends could forgive me?" I assured him that everybody, including God, would forgive him if he sincerely asked.

This was almost more than my emotions could handle. As he gave his life to the Lord, I was thrilled and happy beyond description. At the same time, I felt a load of responsibility to teach him and walk with him through the difficult times that were sure to come. During the next few months, Satan did everything he could to get Alex back. Alex faithfully brought his family to church services and prayer meetings. We were thrilled to see him with a big smile on his face and a Bible under his arm. I recall asking him how he felt. "I don't know how it could get any better," he replied.

As time went by, we started to notice a "cooling off" in Alex's spiritual walk. Then we heard that he was drinking again. Thankfully, he quickly realized he was backsliding and made arrangements to go through the Alcoholics Anonymous program. He did quit his drinking, but as he told me later, God is never mentioned in AA's program. They only speak of a "higher power," and when we call on a higher power, it could be Satan who answers.

When Alex had conquered his drinking problem, he talked of his desire to become a pilot and fly bush planes. My personal opinion was that he was too old to attempt something like that. But he did quite well. He flew a Cessna 185 on pontoons in the summer and skis in the winter. Although he had several mishaps, he mastered the art of flying a bush plane. There were two times when Alex flipped his plane and ended up swimming to shore while his aircraft slowly sank to the bottom of the lake. Alex told me later that God must have had something in mind for him by preserving his life.

Alex's Later Years

Twenty years later Alex's health deteriorated because of the heavy drinking in his past. He was in and out of the hospital almost weekly. He was diabetic and eventually the doctors had to amputate his leg. By this time, Alex's children were also alcoholics—almost worse than he had been. He talked about this to me. He said he had asked them many times to forgive him and to change their ways, but their drinking continued. One of his sons left home and lived on the streets of Toronto, often holding a cup and begging for money. He later moved to Thunder Bay and did the same thing there. He was under the influence of alcohol most of the time. He rarely came to Slate Falls for even a short visit. Chris, another of Alex's sons, was also a heavy drinker and made life miserable for his father.

But there was one bright spot in Alex's family. He had a son named Charley who was a Christian. Charley passed away when he was twenty-two years old. I had always been impressed with Charley. He read and really studied his Bible. I remember one evening in particular. Charley was at our house for the evening and asked for a ride home, which I was happy to do. When we got to his house, he talked and talked, mostly asking questions about Scriptures. I am ashamed to admit it, but I almost told him to go inside because I was too tired to talk any longer.

As Alex's condition worsened, it became clear that he would soon pass on. One night the resident missionary, Duane, was at his bedside in the hospital. It became evident that this might be Alex's last night on earth. Alex asked Duane if he thought he had asked everyone he had wronged for forgiveness. Alex had indeed asked some people for forgiveness. He had even talked to my wife about the situation when we had to leave Slate Falls for a while. He took Edna's hand and gave her a wad of money. With tears in his eyes, he asked, "Can you forgive me for the hard times I caused you?"

Sitting by Alex's bedside, Duane went over some Scriptures about accepting the Lord. Alex looked at the people standing around his bedside in the hospital, smiled, and said in a husky voice, "You know, I am excited to go."

Alex turned to his wife Molly, who had recently become a Christian, and asked, "Is it okay if I go now?" Molly was silent for a bit, then replied, "Yes, it is okay." Shortly thereafter, Alex departed from this life to eternity.

Chapter 16

Incidents and Accidents

Living in the "bush" certainly has its disadvantages, but there is usually a way to make do.

One time our daughter Phyllis had appendicitis, which required chartering a floatplane to fly an hour to a hospital for surgery. Once our son Jeremy broke his arm in a freak snowmobile accident. He missed a turn and crashed into a woodpile. His arm was bent behind the wrist at about a thirty-degree angle. Of course, these things seemed to happen mainly in the evening when flying is impossible until morning, which made for some miserable, painful nights for the patient.

When our children discovered they had head lice, they believed it was the end of the world. Well, not quite! We discovered a cheap fix. Washing the hair in kerosene and rinsing with vinegar worked really well. The kerosene killed the active bugs, and the vinegar dissolved the unhatched eggs.

The Fire

One beautiful fall evening in early November, when the weather had that frosty feel to it, I was doing my evening chores—splitting firewood, filling wood boxes, and carrying water. In other words, the normal routine in a northern setting.

Then I moved on to filling several five-gallon gas cans with fuel. We had a small shanty just for fuel storage. We always tried to have airplane fuel on hand in case some plane was passing by and in need of fuel. The little shanty contained approximately 150 gallons of various kinds of fuel. I was pouring gasoline from one container into another when suddenly, without warning, the can in my hands began to burn. I set the can on the floor and ran for the house. I quickly grabbed a fire extinguisher from behind the door, but by the time I came back to the shanty it was already engulfed in flames. The fire was so severe that I couldn't even get close. Then the fifty-gallon drums began to explode, and as they did, holes burst through the roof and became like orifices shooting fuel to the tops of the trees. Trees sixty feet tall were burning at the tops.

Of course, by this time the whole community had seen or heard the fireworks and had come to help. Many people came with buckets and formed a bucket brigade. The main concern was our house, only fifty feet from the inferno. There was also a log shanty where we kept firewood, and it was starting to burn on the side toward the fire. It seemed like the whole village was there to help.

We had a standby pump in case of a fire, and I was down by the lake trying to get it engaged. But try as I would, I could not get it working. By now it was dark except for the raging fire. Since I was not at the site of the fire, people thought I might be in the fire. A few were even thinking of dashing into the fire to rescue me. Thankfully I showed up before they did that.

The windows of our house on the side of the fire were all broken from the heat. There were fishermen six miles down the lake who heard the explosions, and several people out on boats several miles away sensed the shaking when the barrels exploded.

As undesirable as it was to experience something like this, it made people think. Late into the night, we had people knocking on our door requesting prayer. It made some people think about hell, and others had confessions to share. Through it all, animosities were laid aside, and it showed us that "All things work together for good to them that love God."

A Tragedy

Five community members went to town one day for what they thought was a normal trip. However, such a day is a real test for people who struggle with addiction problems. Five people in a vehicle left Sioux Lookout in the late afternoon. Many questions are still unanswered, but it must have happened after midnight when the driver, who was apparently under the influence of alcohol, missed a bridge that crosses the Broken Mouth River. There were no survivors and no witnesses. However, the following day a passerby happened to see the underside of a vehicle sticking out of the water. Upon further inspection, they discovered that there were people in the vehicle!

The vehicle was pulled out of the water and the bodies removed. This was an awful trauma to work through. I will never forget the feeling I had when we entered the church with five caskets lined up along the walls. It was heartrending to witness the sorrow and hopelessness of relatives as they looked into the caskets.

It is remarkable that in cases like this, everybody, both Christians and non-Christians, are very concerned that the deceased somehow accepted the Lord before they died. We know that these people have all had teaching from the Bible and have some knowledge of accepting the Lord. We also know that the thief on the cross called out to God in his dying hour and was promised forgiveness. But we hastened to warn the people that this was no way to live. Many people die suddenly, in ways that provide no opportunity for repentance. We are thankful that God is the judge and not us.

Snowmobile Problems

We made many trips from Slate Falls to Cat Lake, and often one of our children would go along for the ride. On one of those trips, my daughter Virginia went with me. We left Cat Lake for Slate Falls early in the morning. The weather was not real cold, maybe around zero. We were about halfway through the trip when all at once the engine on our snowmobile started to make strange noises. In a matter of minutes, the engine stopped. It was kaput. The cooling fan had broken, causing it to overheat and then seize up.

I looked at Virginia and asked if she was in the mood to walk thirty miles. She wasn't, and neither was I, but there were no other options. It was over thirty miles to Cat Lake and thirty miles to Slate Falls, so we started to walk. Fortunately, the rest of our family was expecting us to show up in Slate Falls by lunch. When we didn't arrive when expected, they sent two people on snowmobiles to see what was wrong. Virginia and I were overjoyed to hear the snowmobiles coming in the distance. We had probably walked six or eight miles through fairly soft snow.

A Long Journey

The natives still chuckle as they tell of the reaction when Allen and Emma Sommers first set foot in Slate Falls in 1955. At first, parents did not allow their children to be near these white men because they worried that they might be poisoned. Gradually, however, the people began to trust them.

It is to our shame that the natives were skeptical of the white missionaries. They had reason to be. If we look back at the early explorers and their first contact with North American natives, it is not something to be proud of. The first white people were the explorers/hunters who took advantage of the natives in trading. For example, if a native wanted to purchase a gun, the white men would charge the natives a stack of beaver pelts as high as the length of the gun.

The image the natives had of white men was not good. They were "ripped off" on any transaction that was made.

Next came the Anglican missionaries who exploited the natives in a spiritual way. They offered to baptize their babies for a fee, assuring them that their children would now have sure entry into heaven. This only compounded the exploitation begun by the traders.

As the Canadian government began to establish law and order after the French and Indian War, the natives were again caught in the grip of the white men, who were moving in and taking away their homeland. Eventually the Canadian government and the natives signed an agreement, but there were many inconsistencies in this treaty.

As the government established their control on the native lands, they insisted that their children must go to school, so residential schools were established. Since people lived in the bush, this meant the government could take the children away from their parents for as long as seven months at a time. Many of the schools the children were put into were operated by Anglican churches. Many adults relate stories of abuse when they were in these schools.

Not all of the abuse rumors are true, but some are and have had lasting effects on the people. A protest movement was started around twenty years ago and has brought up many old animosities, which is not good. The abused victims were given large sums of money as reconciliation. Many of these victims have gone through awful depression, resulting in alcohol and drug use, violence, and suicide.

One Anglican priest flew an airplane all over the north to baptize children and serve communion to the natives. This priest was later exposed as one of the worst abusers in the whole Northwest Territory. He is now in prison for life.

The government also agreed to provide for the natives' medical services. I am sure the government had no clue what this entailed. The program was easy to take advantage of, and the recipients knew just how to do it. If someone had an alcohol problem, they could easily come to the clinic and tell my wife Edna, who ran the clinic, that they had chest pains. "I think I should go to the hospital," they would tell her. "I think I might be having a heart attack."

What some of them really wanted was the chance to go to town and bring home some alcohol and groceries. It was sometimes hard for Edna to decide if they really needed to see a doctor—whether it was a heart attack or an alcohol attack. She did not want to neglect something serious, but neither did she want to satisfy their thirst with a trip to town.

There is still a general caution among the natives regarding the white man's culture. Many, though, are fast being acclimated into this culture, although this varies from place to place. Slate Falls, in general, is a strong supporter of our mission. Several years ago the community wanted to build a new church. It was very impressive how they supported this. They paid over $100,000 for building materials. Our churches furnished most of the labor, but the community paid the bills. It's encouraging that the native people want a Christian presence in their community.

A Troubled Past

It was difficult to follow a timeline in this book, and the stories overlap at times. Edna and I, with our three children, lived in Slate Falls for three years. We then felt our children should have youth to fellowship with, so we made plans to return home to Holmes County, Ohio.

Once we were back home, Ivan Cook led the teaching in the church in Slate Falls. He did very well in leading the church, but it became too heavy a load for him, so the community asked us to come back. For a number of years we had staff living and working there.

In 2001, with our children now adults, Edna and I moved to Slate Falls again and served another three years. This was when we spent three or four months at a time during the winters at Cat Lake.

Even now, though we are not directly serving at Slate Falls, we have an established mission staff there and aim to visit there once a year.

We are planting seeds. Not all of them will grow, but some will. God never requires us to see the success of our work. He only requires us to be faithful. We believe souls were saved in Slate Falls, and that makes our work there successful to us. No, multitudes were not saved, but one soul is worth more than the whole world. If we only count success by a large church assembly and membership, we did not see that. But there are several faithful members there, and we have seen some growth. For that, we are thankful. We pray that as time goes on, more people will be open to the Gospel of Jesus.

Part Three

Other Travel Adventures

Chapter 17

An Unforgettable Trip

It was 1991, and our good friends Freeman and Amanda Miller had decided to join us to go visit Norman and Karen Troyer, who were serving in Ukraine. This was just after the fall of communism, and the way people did things in the former Soviet Union had not changed much. Corruption was still a way of life, and people were cautious in their dealings with others.

We, on the other hand, had grown up among honest people, and as a result we tended to believe that the people around us were also trustworthy. This trip showed us that this isn't always the case.

Our journey first took us to Poland, where we visited a mission and also a concentration camp where thousands of Jews were killed during Hitler's occupation. Our plan was to be there for one weekend and then travel by train to Kiev, Ukraine, where we would spend a week with Norman and Karen. We also planned to visit various places in the former communist countries. The train we were traveling on left Warsaw, Poland, at 8:00 p.m. on a Sunday evening.

As we were preparing to go to the train station, the Polish Mission informed us that we would need to take an interpreter along because the agents did not speak English, and we could not speak Russian. I was not too happy with the idea because I had done a fair amount of traveling, and we had always managed to communicate. But, rather reluctantly, we hired an interpreter named Juan to go with us. We would then pay for his return back to Poland.

It was already dark when we boarded the train, and we were ready to go to bed in our sleeper car. We had one booth for the four of us. Edna and I would sleep on the top bunk, with Freeman and Amanda below us. Juan helped us find our booth, and we assumed he would also find a spot for himself somewhere on the train. The train was just starting to move, and we were already dozing, when there was a knock on our door. There stood Juan. He came right on in and deposited himself on the floor beside our bed. Then he began talking. He talked and talked, explaining how he might be part Jewish—at least he hoped he was. We soon decided that this could go on all night, so we got out some snacks to chew on while we listened to him talk.

Sometime later a conductor came to our booth to let us know we needed to get off the train while they stopped at the border. Russia had set up their train tracks so that other countries could not readily use them. Therefore, whenever the train crossed the border, they had to adjust the wheels on the train to fit the tracks in the communist bloc. This took some time at the border, and for some reason they wanted us off the train.

It was November, so it was cold with snow on the ground. As we stepped outside, a gust of freezing wind hit us. We started to wonder about this whole setup. We didn't understand why we had to leave the train. We huddled and shivered, wondering what would happen next. Then we noticed another train parked nearby, so we decided to get on that train to keep warm. Soon a lady who could speak English came and asked us what we are doing. We couldn't give her a very good answer!

While sitting in the train, we noticed about a dozen soldiers in a little grove of trees up ahead. They had a big army truck, the kind with six wheels and a round canvas top that was open at the back. It was now midnight, and the soldiers kept watching us and laughing. Finally one of them came our way and motioned for us to follow, then to get into the back of the truck. It was no small feat to get our wives on the back of a Russian army truck that was four feet high.

There were benches along the sides of the truck, and all the soldiers were seated on the benches. One of the crew said in broken English, "Sit here, American." Our wives were squished in between the soldiers, but there was no room for me, so I knelt down in the middle of the truck bed. I decided kneeling might be the best position to be in anyway, considering our situation.

With a roar, we began driving through forests and then through a small village. We spoke to one another, confident that our "colleagues" could not understand us. We also wondered where Juan was—not to mention that we had left our snacks and the women's coverings on the train.

Riding on an army truck in Russia was quite unusual, and in our conversation we remarked that if this had happened several years before this, we would definitely have been headed for Siberia. In a sense, it was a funny thought, and yet it wasn't.

After driving who knows where, they dropped us off at a very small office. There was an officer there, obviously a dispatcher of some sort. Inside the office was an entire wall of plugs. The officer would take the wire he had in his hand and talk into the mouthpiece, or I should say scream into it. Then he'd plug it into one hole, then another, with seemingly no response. We finally got the idea across to the soldiers that we wanted to get our visas, so they took us to another building to get them. We had been told that each visa would cost around $15, but for us that night, each visa cost $50. We reasoned that we were so far from home that we might as well pay it and not argue. Then, lo and behold, there sat Juan in the next office we came to, with all our precious snacks and the women's coverings. He seemed to be enjoying his role, whatever it was.

Soon another officer came in and announced, by pointing to his watch, that the train had left already. Juan was not concerned. "Tomorrow will be another train," he said.

We then made it clear that we needed to get to Kiev that day—not tomorrow. Norman and Karen were expecting us, and we had no way to inform them of our delay. "Is there another village where we could get a train and still get to Kiev?" I asked.

"Sure," they replied. "We can take you there by taxi."

"How much will it cost?" we asked.

With very little hesitation, the answer came back—$50 each.

(Clearly, this was a familiar number to them.) We agreed, knowing we had no other options at this point, and walked outside to a tiny car with a smiling driver. Juan seemed to know the driver personally. But how could they expect four full-sized people to fit in the back seat, plus all our luggage? With some extensive pushing and shoving, we finally crammed into the car. Remember, this was wintertime in Ukraine, where there are no snowplows. The snow was packed and frozen with potholes everywhere. I suppose the little car was bottomed out with all the weight.

We finally arrived at a little village and pulled up to the train station while Juan went in to get the tickets. It did not take long for him to return, but with no tickets. With a rather sheepish grin, he said, "We just missed the train."

We began racking our brains as to what to do. Since we were already dead-tired, we decided to get a hotel and try again in the morning. We asked Juan about a hotel, so he checked with the clerk. After getting directions, we drove to a rather dumpy-looking building where Juan dashed in. He came back and informed us that there was room.

Our first question was, "What is the cost?"

We weren't surprised when he replied, "$50 each!"

Since it was almost morning anyway, we were hesitant to spend all that money for just a few hours. After a little discussion, we asked if there was any bus service to Kiev. Thankfully, there was, but it was several hours away. We did not even ask how much it would cost, fearing the answer would be $50 each.

It was midmorning by the time we arrived at the bus station. And now there was another problem: after bouncing around for so long, we needed a restroom—and the facilities were anything but high-tech. Our wives knew very little about squatty potties, but they learned fast.

We finally got on the bus—by early afternoon. The bus was crammed full. By the time we got to Kiev, I had people sitting on my lap. As we approached the big city of Kiev, it was evening. Norman and Karen had been expecting us that morning, so they had no idea where their visitors were. They had gone to the train station several times with no success in finding us.

When we arrived in Kiev, it was around 7:00 p.m. and dark. The city was not lit up like American cities, and I noticed that Juan had a worried look on his face. He kept looking out the window of the bus. Suddenly he told the bus driver to stop. "Follow me!" he told us. "Quick!"

It was a challenge to find our luggage and get off the bus quickly with it being so full. We finally made it off and stood beside the road in the snow, shivering till our teeth were chattering. We looked around for Juan, but he had disappeared again. It wasn't long till he came running back and told us to follow him. Dragging our bags through the snow was not easy, and by this time we were exhausted.

Imagine the situation if you can: It's very dark, and we are dragging our luggage through the snow. We're also trying to keep track of Juan, who has no luggage himself and doesn't seem to care how we manage with ours. He is taking us cross country to the area where he thinks Norman and Karen might live. The ground is covered with about six inches of snow and we have no boots.

Finally we came to some apartment buildings, and Juan told us he is not sure which building Norman and Karen lived in, and we should just wait until he found the right one. There were six drab concrete buildings, and they all looked alike. Juan kept going up one elevator and then another.

After we had been searching for about an hour, Norman and Karen suddenly came walking toward us. They had made another trip to the train station to look for us and were just returning home. Needless to say, we were overjoyed to see them. We went up to their apartment and were soon enjoying some food Karen prepared for us. We encouraged Juan to go to bed, and he did. We were almost too tired to sleep, but we did the best we could.

In the morning, Juan came out of his room and ate breakfast with us. He was preparing to take the train back to Warsaw. We gave him a generous amount of money for his efforts, as well as the train fare for his return. We also packed some food for him, then bade him goodbye. By this time, we were aware that this whole scenario was a setup to clean out our wallets. We were relieved to see him leave.

An hour later there was a knock on the door. There stood Juan. He said that the strangest thing had happened. While he was waiting for his train, he had decided to get a haircut. He had parked his bag, which included the money for his train fare, in a corner, and while he was getting a haircut somebody stole his bag! Now he needed more food and some money for the train fare! How creative can one be? It was then very clear that we were set up. To get rid of him, we gave him some money but made it clear that there would be no more!

In hindsight, we would have done better with no interpreter. Thankfully, we did have just enough money left to get us home again. Not all was in vain—we had an enjoyable visit and even learned a few things about traveling.

Chapter 18

Visas for Romanians

For forty years now Edna and I have hosted tours to Israel and Europe. The European tours feature areas where our Amish and Mennonite forefathers lived until they emigrated to America. We had our first tour in 1979, and on average we have had one tour per year. We have also led several tours to Egypt, Jordan, Romania, Ukraine, and Turkey.

On one of our tours, we had a request from twelve Romanians who wished to join us. I soon discovered that Romanians were not readily granted visas to travel in Israel. There seemed to be a long-standing political issue somewhere. In order to get the visa issue underway, I made a few phone calls to the Romanian Embassy in Washington,

D.C. It was very difficult to find someone who would help in such matters, but finally I spoke with a lady who at least gave us some answers. She informed us that, for starters, they would need the Romanian passports in hand. The problem was, the passports were in Romania. How could I get twelve passports to America so quickly?

Our friend Silvia was in Romania at the time, so we were able to make contact fairly directly. She discovered that there was indeed someone from America visiting Romania who would leave for America the very next day. So in a very short time, I had twelve passports in my hands. *Good start,* I thought. I contacted the lady in D.C. again, and she promised if I could bring the passports to her in Washington, she would issue the visas. We made an appointment for a day and time when she would be available.

Edna and I flew to Washington, D.C., on the designated day and time. We found the embassy easily enough, but when we asked to see the woman with whom we had made the appointment, they told us, "Sorry, she is not working today."

The gentleman we spoke to at the embassy was very cooperative as I explained what we needed. He asked if I would be willing to take full responsibility to make sure all twelve travelers returned to Romania after the tour. He said I would need to write a letter on an official letterhead for our tour. I actually had such paperwork. However, I didn't have a computer or typewriter handy, so how could I produce an official-looking letter? He told us that there was a Kinkos office down the street about two blocks. We could write our letter on a computer at Kinkos and bring it back to him for approval.

In that day and age, many people were not computer smart—I certainly wasn't. But somehow I managed to write a fairly official-looking letter. I took the letter back to the gentleman at the embassy. At this point, we were in a race with time, with less than two weeks until our departure date.

The gentleman at the embassy looked at the letter, studied it thoroughly, and pointed out one paragraph he did not like. "You better go back to Kinkos and do it over," he said. We rushed there and back, and the second version was approved. The man looked at me over the top of his glasses and told me to pack up all the passports along with the letter, take the package to a FedEx station, and send it overnight delivery to the embassy in Bucharest. Wow!

Time was fleeting, and by now it was late afternoon, but we did manage to get the package shipped. It took many greenbacks, but I had fulfilled my duty.

Edna and I flew home the next day. I couldn't help but wonder how this package of passports was going to get into the right hands in Romania. But Bill Mullet, a friend of mine from the States who had lived in Romania for several years, assured me. "You will be surprised what happens when Romanians pray," he said.

I waited a few days to make sure the passports had been received, then I called the embassy in Romania to ask about them.

"Call back tomorrow!" they responded. I didn't tell them how few tomorrows I had left. This went on for several days. Meanwhile, the travelers in Romania were kept informed of the communication going on.

We were just about at the end of the rope for time. I kept calling the embassy and their answer was always, "We know nothing about it." It was also clear that they didn't care. However, they did say, "The only person who would know anything about it is a lady by the name of Espy. But you can't call her; she doesn't answer phone calls." This seemed like death to a vision!

One evening when I went to bed, I just told the Lord, "This is your project. Do whatever needs to be done. If there is a time when Espy would accept a phone call, please wake me up." I went to bed completely at ease.

Let me stop here for a moment. You need to know something about me to really appreciate this. I am a deep sleeper, and I never wake up at night.

I went to bed that night as usual, falling asleep immediately. Sometime later I woke up. Groggily I looked at the clock on my bedside. It said 2:00 a.m. Instantly I remembered my prayer. I went to the phone and called Romania. I spoke to a lady. "Espy is not here," she said. "And if she would be, she wouldn't answer the phone." Then she said, "Wait!"

After a minute, another voice came on the line. "Hello, I am Espy. What can I do for you?"

I was almost speechless. I explained the whole situation to her. She answered, "I have this package from FedEx. It has been here beside my desk, and I had no idea what it was for." Opening it, she said there were twelve passports inside. I asked her what the next move was to procure the visas, and she said I would need to have all these passport holders come to the embassy the next morning. I negotiated with her, reminding her that these people were mostly from Suceava, and they would need to take the train from Suceava to Bucharest. I asked if there was any way we could send two people in the morning to transact the visas. Espy agreed to that.

The next morning three of the twelve travelers arrived early at the embassy. The embassy's system was such that they had the doors to the embassy open until they had the number of people they could process in a day. The people who came for the visas were the last three to be admitted. The doors were closed right behind them.

If you are reading this, please don't ever think God is not interested in the little things. He is even capable of waking a sleepyhead like me. God knew exactly when Espy would arrive at work, and He knew what minute she would walk down the hall past the receptionist who was on the phone with me.

The trip was a wonderful tour for the Romanians. They felt so blessed and kept praising the Lord throughout the tour.

Epilogue

There—you have read a book written by an author who has never written one before. And if it hadn't been for all the help and encouragement from my wife Edna, I would never have gotten it done! The first question people ask us about our time in Slate Falls is, "Didn't you get homesick?" But the joy we felt in feeling that this was where God wanted us eased much of our sadness. There were numerous "little miracles" that showed us God was in control—so much so that we assumed He could take care of any situation that arose.

People often wonder what the measure of success is in endeavors like this. As I've mentioned before, we must remember that God never requires us to see the success of our work. He only requires us to be faithful, and that itself is success.

As we look back and consider the labors of our mission projects, we do see some positive changes. God shall have all the honor.

We hope this book will motivate people to trust the Lord in a deeper way, and when God calls we hope you will answer. But let me be quick to say that we do not need to go to another country to be a witness. We can be a witness wherever we are! God calls people to all kinds of places and projects. God uses ordinary people to accomplish His work. Consider the disciples of Jesus. They were ordinary and diverse, but they accomplished the work of the Lord.

If we need something to motivate us, consider Luke 16:19-31. Here Christ uses the account of the rich man and a beggar named Lazarus, who both died. The rich man, having been sent to hell, was in awful pain. He saw the beggar comforted in Abraham's arms in heaven and requested just one drop of water from them. But Abraham told the rich man that his decision had been made. He could have changed his destiny, but now it was too late. Let us read this and do all we can to "pull people from the fire."

Also consider Revelation 7:9-10:

> After this I beheld, and, lo, a great multitude, which no man could number, of all nations, and kindreds, and people, and tongues, stood before the throne, and before the Lamb, clothed with white robes, and palms in their hands; and cried with a loud voice, saying, Salvation to our God which sitteth upon the throne, and unto the Lamb.

Let us help people—whether in our own neighborhoods or in remote villages around the world—join that great multitude.

About the Author

Edwin and Edna Troyer live near Sugarcreek, Ohio, and are members of the New Order Amish Church.

They have three children, all of whom are now married. They enjoy spending time with their ten grandchildren and three great-grandchildren.

Edwin spent many years in the cabinetry trade where he become skilled in building sturdy furniture. After their stay in Canada, Edwin became involved in taking groups to Israel to show them the land of the Bible. His son-in-law, Duane Troyer, took over this job in 2018. Edwin worked in the travel department at the CAM Berlin office from 2004 to 2016, where he purchased many a ticket for overseas staff. He loves working with people and has gotten to know many through the years.

Edwin would be happy to hear from readers and can be contacted through Christian Aid Ministries at 330-893-2428 or by direct email at edwinandedna@outlook.com

About Christian Aid Ministries

Christian Aid Ministries was founded in 1981 as a nonprofit, tax-exempt 501(c)(3) organization. Its primary purpose is to provide a trustworthy and efficient channel for Amish, Mennonite, and other conservative Anabaptist groups and individuals to minister to physical and spiritual needs around the world. This is in response to the command to ". . . do good unto all men, especially unto them who are of the household of faith" (Galatians 6:10).

CAM supporters provide millions of pounds of food, clothing, Bibles, medicines, and other aid each year. Supporters' funds also help victims of disasters in the U.S. and abroad, put up Gospel billboards in the U.S., and provide Biblical teaching and self-help resources.

CAM's main purposes for providing aid are to help and encourage God's people and bring the Gospel to a lost and dying world.

The Way to God and Peace

We live in a world contaminated by sin. Sin is anything that goes against God's holy standards. When we do not follow the guidelines that God our Creator gave us, we are guilty of sin. Sin separates us from God, the source of life.

Since the time when the first man and woman, Adam and Eve, sinned in the Garden of Eden, sin has been universal. The Bible says that we all have "sinned and come short of the glory of God" (Romans 3:23). It also says that the natural consequence for that sin is eternal death, or punishment in an eternal hell: "Then when lust hath conceived, it bringeth forth sin: and sin, when it is finished, bringeth forth death" (James 1:15).

But we do not have to suffer eternal death in hell. God provided forgiveness for our sins through the death of His only Son, Jesus Christ. Because Jesus was perfect and without sin, He could die in our place. "For God so loved the world that he gave his only begotten Son, that whosoever believeth in him should not perish, but have everlasting life" (John 3:16).

A sacrifice is something given to benefit someone else. It costs the giver greatly. Jesus was God's sacrifice. Jesus' death takes away the penalty of sin for all those who accept this sacrifice and truly repent of their sins. To repent of sins means to be truly sorry for and turn away from the things we have done that have violated God's standards (Acts 2:38; 3:19).

Jesus died, but He did not remain dead. After three days, God's Spirit miraculously raised Him to life again. God's Spirit does something similar in us. When we receive Jesus as our sacrifice and repent of our sins, our hearts are changed. We become spiritually alive! We develop new desires and attitudes (2 Corinthians 5:17). We begin to make choices that please God (1 John 3:9). If we do fail and commit sins, we can ask God for forgiveness. "If we confess our sins, he is faithful and just to forgive us our sins, and to cleanse us from all unrighteousness" (1 John 1:9).

Once our hearts have been changed, we want to continue growing spiritually. We will be happy to let Jesus be the Master of our lives and will want to become more like Him. To do this, we must meditate on God's Word and commune with God in prayer. We will testify to others of this change by being baptized and sharing the good news of God's victory over sin and death. Fellowship with a faithful group of believers will strengthen our walk with God (1 John 1:7).